Sub-Machine Guns and Automatic Rifles

WW2 FACT FILES

PETER CHAMBERLAIN and TERRY GANDER

World War 2 saw the emergence of the personal automatic weapon: the sub-machine gun and the automatic or assault rifle. These weapons enabled the individual foot soldier vastly to increase his available fire-power with the resultant changes in his tactics and battlefield role. In 1939 the full potential of the sub-machine gun had yet to be realised by many nations but Germany had ready the MP38 which was soon countered by the crude Sten Guns and the American M3 'Grease Gun'. Also in this Fact File are the notorious Thompson guns and the numerous Russian sub-machine guns. From the sub-machine gun concept grew the automatic rifle with its new range of ammunition specially produced for the new weapon that could fire single-shot or full automatic up to combat ranges and yet still light enough for the average infantryman to carry and use. Foremost among the new 'assault rifles' were the German StG 44 and FG42, but Russian and other designs are covered. Also included in this Fact File is a section on flamethrowers.

WORLD WAR 2 FACT FILES

Sub-Machine Guns and Automatic Rifles

PETER CHAMBERLAIN
AND TERRY GANDER

Published by Arco Publishing Company, Inc.
219 Park Avenue South, New York, 10003

Library of Congress Cataloging in Publication Data

Chamberlain, Peter.
Submachine guns and automatic rifles.

(World War II fact files)
1. Submachine guns. 2. Rifles. 3. World War, 1939-1945 – Supplies. I. Gander, T. J., joint author. II. Title.
UF620.A2C443 623.4'424 76-28423
ISBN 0-668-04013-0

Printed in Great Britain

$4.95

Arco Publishing Company, Inc.
New York

Introduction

During the Great War the tactical role of the Infantry was dictated by the overall supremacy of the machine gun. The Second World War was also very much a war of the machine gun but during that conflict the infantryman was no longer completely subordinate to that weapon for his individual firepower increased dramatically with the use of the sub-machine gun. Although the first sub-machine guns were in use during the last part of the First World War the first conflict in which they took part on a major scale was the Spanish Civil War. There, as after, the sub-machine gun proved itself to be an indispensable weapon in the close confines of trench fighting, the close confusion of night attacks and the stealth of patrols and raiding parties. Those who took part in the Spanish Civil War began to arm themselves with large numbers of sub-machine guns, but those who stood apart from that conflict failed to realise the importance of the sub-machine gun and virtually ignored it as a viable weapon. Thus in 1939 Germany, Italy and Russia were making plans to produce large numbers of sub-machine guns. The United Kingdom and the USA had none and, what was more important, had no plans to obtain any.

It was at this point that one of the most important points of the sub-machine gun came to light. During 1940 it was realised that the sub-machine gun could be turned out in large numbers by simple production methods and a minimum of cost and effort. After 1940 the sub-machine gun was no longer a complex, well-made weapon built along the traditional lines of the trained gunsmith. It became a crude ugly little weapon knocked up by virtually untrained machinists at any place where machine tools could be set up. The numbers turned out during the Second World War were enormous. One reference has calculated that from 1939 to 1945 well over twenty million sub-machine guns were turned out by the combatants engaged in what was the most costly war ever fought. These huge numbers of readily-available weapons not only gave the average soldier an increase in firepower, they also changed his tactics. The sub-machine gun, by definition, fires a short-range pistol round, and this short range meant that close quarter tactics became the rule. Shock and surprise contact fighting took the place of long range combat, and the rise of the night attack coupled with the rapid movement of large bodies of troops by mechanical transport dictated the course of many of the later battles of World War 2. It was not only on the battlefield that the sub-machine gun made its mark. The hit-and-run activities of the Commando-type raiding party were a constant feature of the new combat tactics, and in the undercover world of the resistance fighter or partisan, the sub-machine gun became an essential part of everyday existence.

Perhaps the best example of the change made on tactics by the sub-machine gun can be seen in the example set by the Russian Army. The German invasion of 1941 not only cost them large amounts of equipment and manpower, it also removed much of their industrial capacity. New armies had to be raised and equipped and the Russian answer was the PPSh41. This simple, unlovely weapon was turned out in millions by simple machines in a multitude of odd locations. In action it proved reliable and efficient, but its lack of range dictated the use of the close-contact fighting coupled with massed shock tactics that made the Red Army virtually unstoppable. The PPSh became a trademark of the Russian soldier in the same way that the German MP40 is still associated with German militarism. Of all the sub-machine guns mentioned in this Fact File the MP40 is perhaps the most important as it demonstrated the way all future sub-machine gun design was to follow. Its forebear, the MP38, was designed along conventional lines in that it used the time-honoured methods of construction and assembly. These methods were costly in time and machines, so the MP40 with its simple stampings, lack of finish and overall simplicity was revolutionary. From it came a whole range of designs that took the basic concept to produce such weapons as the Sten, the American M3 and the Australian Owen. Sub-machine guns based on the MP40 were even made in 'back yard' workshops – the Italian Variara is perhaps one of the best examples, and it demonstrated the way that weapon production was to follow in such corners of the world as China.

Coupled with the growth in infantry firepower that the sub-machine gun produced was the increasing role of the self-loading, or automatic rifle. The experiences of the Great War showed the need for some form of self-loading rifle with perhaps the facility to fire fully automatic when needed. Some designs were produced but by 1939 only one, the American M1 Garand, was in service. The main problem faced by the self-loading rifle designer was that most service ammunition was quite simply too powerful for light automatic weapons. The stresses produced by the normal rifle cartridge dictated that any self-loading rifle, and especially one that could fire automatic, was too heavy for normal service use. Rifle cartridges were produced with the need for long range combat in mind, but despite the fact that combat experience in the Great War showed that the great majority of 'fire fights' took place at relatively short ranges of under 400 metres, most combatant nations retained the powerful cartridges they had so carefully stockpiled. As a result, most of the self-loading rifles issued during the Second World War were less than successful. The two exceptions that used normal ammunition were the American Garand and the German FG42. The Garand was used as a self-loading rifle only, but the FG42 was in many ways one of the most remarkable smallarms designs of the Second World War. After 1945 many of its features were used in other designs but it made little change to the tactical scene as its precise tactical role was never defined (it was usually used as a light machine gun) and anyway it was never produced in very large numbers.

The way ahead was shown by the German MP43 family. This weapon used a new round that was specifically designed for the close-quarter fighting dictated by the growing use of the sub-machine gun and mobile mechanised warfare. As ever, the Germans analysed combat experience to evolve a new 7.92 mm kurz (short) round suited to the needs of modern warfare. A weapon firing this round could be constructed to fire fully automatic without the massive metal assemblies usually needed for conventional rounds, and the new rifle could also be made using the experience gained on the sub-machine gun assembly lines. Thus the MP43 and its later versions used steel stampings and a minimum of complex machined parts. Once in service the MP43 was used in such a way that it soon demonstrated that a new type of weapon had emerged. This weapon was the modern assault rifle. The assault rifle not only increased the firepower available to a section commander, it increased the offensive impact that infantry could produce. This, coupled with mobile warfare was to further revolutionise infantry tactics, but the eventual form these tactics will take has, even now, yet to be fully determined.

Flame-throwers. Flame-throwing equipments were first used by the Germans against British troops in July 1916; following this, portable flame-throwers, which were either one or two-man loads, were developed by all belligerents and used throughout the war.

During the inter-war period Britain and the United States devoted little attention to flame-thrower research and development, the flame-thrower to all intents and purpose being written off as a weapon of no military importance.

Other nations did not concur in this appraisal; they were used by the Italian Army in Abyssinia and the Spanish Civil War, and later by the German Army in Poland, in their attack on the Belgium fort of Eben Emael and during the drive through the Low Countries and France.

In 1940 the British and the United States armies took steps towards the development of portable flame-throwers and various equipments were developed.

Photo Credits
Bruno Benvenuti
Dr Nicolas Pignato
K.R. Pawlas
Ian Hogg
C.H. Yust
Imperial War Museum
Bundesarchiv
T. Gander
US Official

AUSTRALIA

Machine Carbine, 9 mm Austen, Mark 1

DATA
CALIBRE 9 mm 0.354 in
LENGTH–BUTT EXTENDED 844.5 mm 33.25 in
LENGTH–BUTT FOLDED 559 mm 22 in
LENGTH OF BARREL 198 mm 7.8 in
WEIGHT 3.97 kg 8.75 lb
M.V. 366 m/s 1200 ft/sec
CYCLIC RATE OF FIRE 500 rpm
MAGAZINE CAPACITY 28 rounds

When Australia found herself with the Pacific War almost on her coastline, her army was small and short of modern weapons. The need for some form of sub-machine gun was particularly severe and the UK was in no position to supply any. Some Thompson sub-machine guns were procured but local production was the answer in the form of the Austen, an amalgamation of two successful designs, the Sten and the MP40. The Sten contributed the feed, barrel and receiver along with the trigger mechanism while the MP40 contributed the folding metal butt and the protected mainspring. Production of the Austen started in mid-1941 at Melbourne and continued until some 20,000 had been produced by 1945. A Mark 2 version was produced in very small numbers.

Austin Mk.1 with folding stock extended

Machine Carbine, 9 mm Owen, Mark 1

DATA (Mark 1/43)
CALIBRE 9 mm 0.354 in
LENGTH 813 mm 32 in
LENGTH OF BARREL 250 mm 9.85 in
WEIGHT 4 kg 8.8 lb
M.V. 419 m/s 1375 ft/sec
CYCLIC RATE OF FIRE 680-700 rpm
MAGAZINE CAPACITY 33 rounds

The Owen sub-machine was designed by a Lt. Evelyn Owen, and went into production at Newcastle, New South Wales in November 1940. It remained in production until September 1944 by which time some 45,000 had been made. The Owen soon proved itself a very sturdy and popular weapon. The bolt was protected against mud and dirt and the overall construction was very robust and reliable. Perhaps the most easily recognisable feature of the Owen was its overhead vertical magazine which ensured a good reliable feed and this feature helped to make the Owen gun more acceptable to the troops in the field (and jungle) rather than the Sten, Thompson or Austen. There were three main versions. First came the Mark 1/42, recognisable by the cooling fins on the barrel. Next came the lighter Mark 1/43 with the cooling fins omitted, and the Mark 1/44 could be fitted with a bayonet. All three Marks had an easily removed barrel held in place by a quick release plunger over the barrel, a feature not often found in sub-machine guns. A Mark 2 version was not approved for production.

Owen Mk.1/42 with metal frame

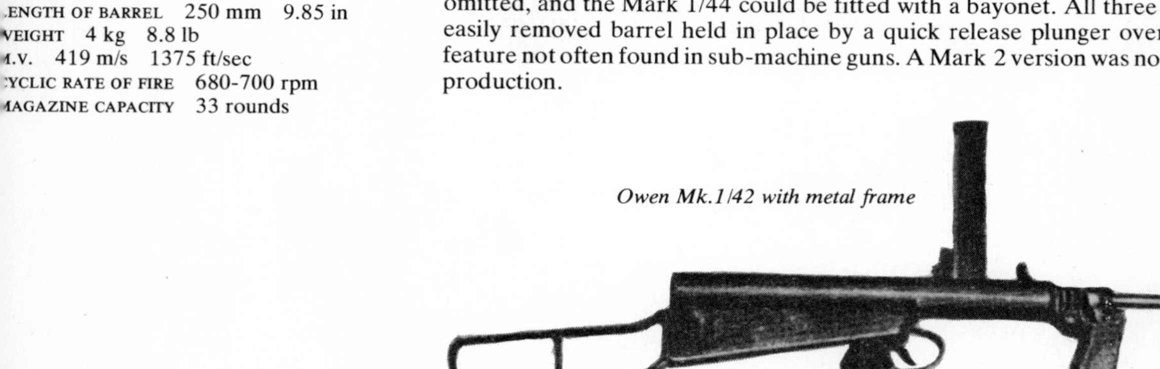

Owen Mk.1/43, note absence of cooling ring on barrel and the modified fram

Australian infantryman in New Guinea, armed with Owen Mk.1/42 with wooden stock

AUSTRIA

Steyr-Solothurn S1-100

The Versailles Treaty of 1919 imposed limitations on the design of automati weapons upon German designers and manufacturers. This was circumvented b Rheinmetall by their purchase of the Swiss Solothurn arms concern, which in tur took an interest in the Austrian Osterreichische Waffenfabrik-Gesellschaft based a Steyr. This conglomerate produced several automatic weapons, one of which was th S1-100 sub-machine gun. The S1-100 was a very well designed and well finishe weaion that was taken over by the Austrian Police and Army as one of their standar weapons. Many were sold to South American states and other customers wer Portugal and Japan (small numbers only). The Austrian Army used the S1-100 as th MP34, and after the German take-over it became the MP34(ö). Overall, the desig of the S1-100 was obviously affected by the MP18/1, but it had several odd desig points, one of which was the magazine filling slot on the magazine housing. A rang of accessories was available including several barrel lengths and a tripod mounting During World War 2 the MP34(ö) was extensively used by military police an second-line units of the Wehrmacht. One further oddity of this weapon was that i could be encountered in three versions, all in 9 mm calibre. Up to 1939 the produc tion version was delivered in 9 mm Mauser. After 1939 this was changed to 9 mn Parabellum, but a further complication was the version for the Austrian Police whicl was produced to take the 9 mm Steyr round. All three versions were in service wit German police and military police units.

DATA

CALIBRE 9 mm 0.354 in
LENGTH 85
mm 33.5 in
LENGTH OF BARREL 196 mm 7.75 in
WEIGHT 4.04 kg 8.9 lb
M.V. 381 m/s 1250 ft/sec
CYCLIC RATE OF FIRE 650 rpm
MAGAZINE CAPACITY 32 rounds

M.P 34 (ö) in service with the Wehrmacht

Steyr-Solothurn SI-100 (M.P 34)

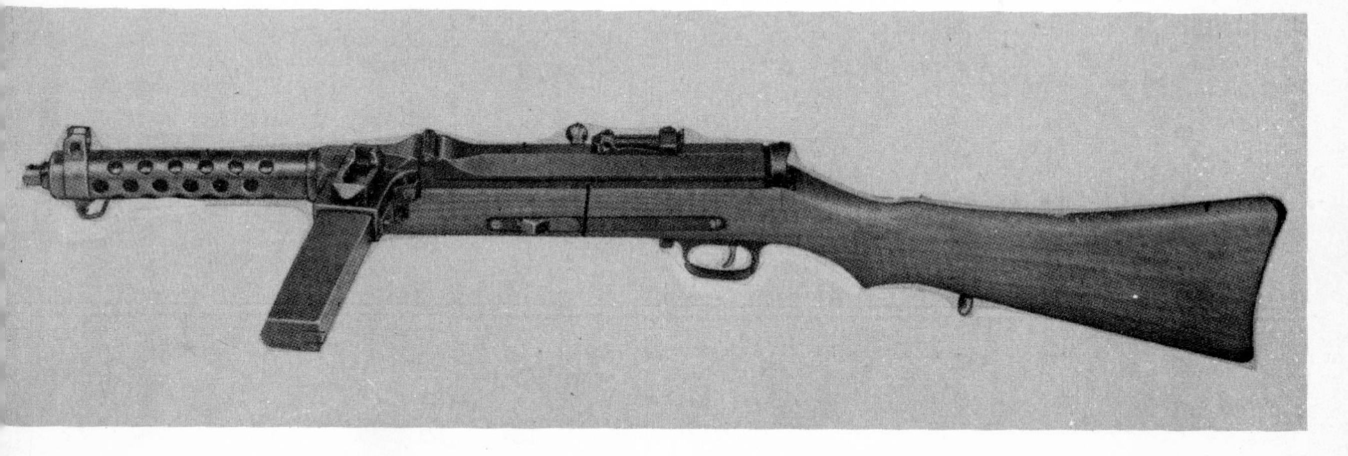

Kulometna Pistole
ZK vz.383

DATA
CALIBRE 9 mm 0.354 in
LENGTH 900 mm 35.4 in
LENGTH OF BARREL 325 mm 12.8 in
WEIGHT 4.27 kg 9.4 lb
M.V. 381 m/s 1250 ft/sec
CYCLIC RATE OF FIRE 500 or 700 rpm
MAGAZINE CAPACITY 30 rounds

CZECHOSLOVAKIA

Kulometna Pistole ZK vz.383

The ZK383 (or vz.383) was designed by Josef and Frantisek Koucky in 1933 and put into production at Brno soon after. It remained in production until 1948. The ZK383 was a very well made weapon with several unusual features not the least of which was a 0.375 lb (0.17 kg) weight that could be fitted to the bolt to vary the rate of fire. Another oddity was a folding bipod which was discarded on the vz.383P 'police' model, and the post-war vz.383H had a folding magazine. A quick-change barrel was fitted. The ZK383 was adopted by the Czech Army but after 1939 all production was directed toward German use, where the type was used by the Waffen SS. Most of the war-time models carried the marking vz.9 The ZK383 was also the standard Bulgarian sub-machine gun, and numbers were sold in South America.

FINLAND

Konepistooli m/31

Development of the sub-machine gun that was to become almost universally known as the 'Suomi' can be traced back to 1922. The first production model to emerge from this line was the m/26 chambered for the 7.63 mm Mauser cartridge but in 1931 the m/31 was produced in 9 mm Parabellum. In this form it became one of the most influential sub-machine gun designs as it greatly influenced Russian weapon development. The m/31 was a very well designed and manufactured weapon. It was licence-made in Sweden, Switzerland and Denmark, and large numbers were sold to such nations as Norway. For a weapon of its type the m/31 was very heavy as all its components were virtually machined from solid metal, and it had a very long barrel which had the advantage of giving a higher degree of accuracy than other weapons in the sub-machine gun family. Overall the m/31 was a very successful though expensive smallarm. Numbers were made for the Danish Army by Madsen as the M.42, and numbers of these came to be used by the Germans as the 9 mm MP 746(d), although their use seems to have been restricted to troops based in Denmark. Some were doubtless captured in Norway but no record seems to have survived of these.

DATA
CALIBRE 9 mm 0.354 in
LENGTH 870 mm 34.25 in
LENGTH OF BARREL 31u.5 mm 12.5 in
WEIGHT 4.676 kg 10.3 lb
M.V. 399 m/s 1310 ft/sec
CYCLIC RATE OF FIRE 900 rpm
MAGAZINE CAPACITY 20, 50 or 71 rounds

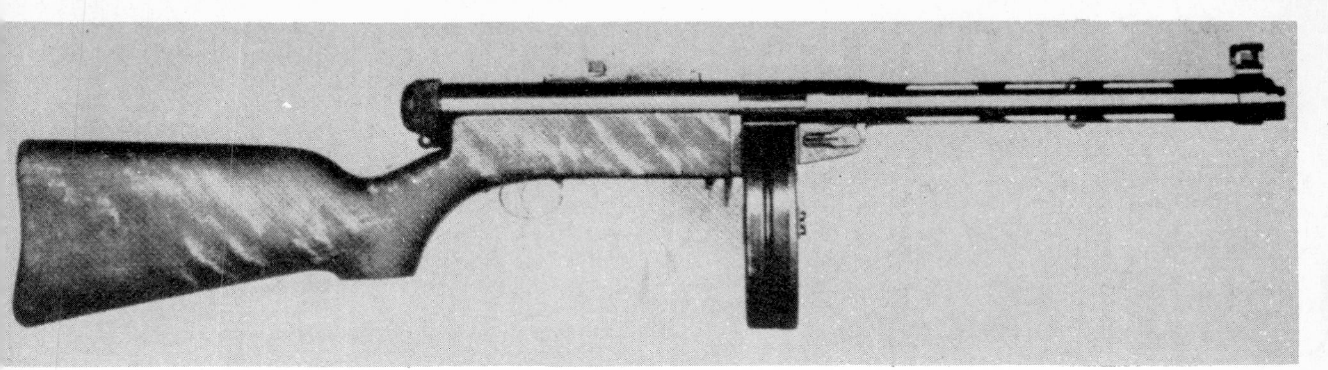

Konepistooli m/31 with drum magazine

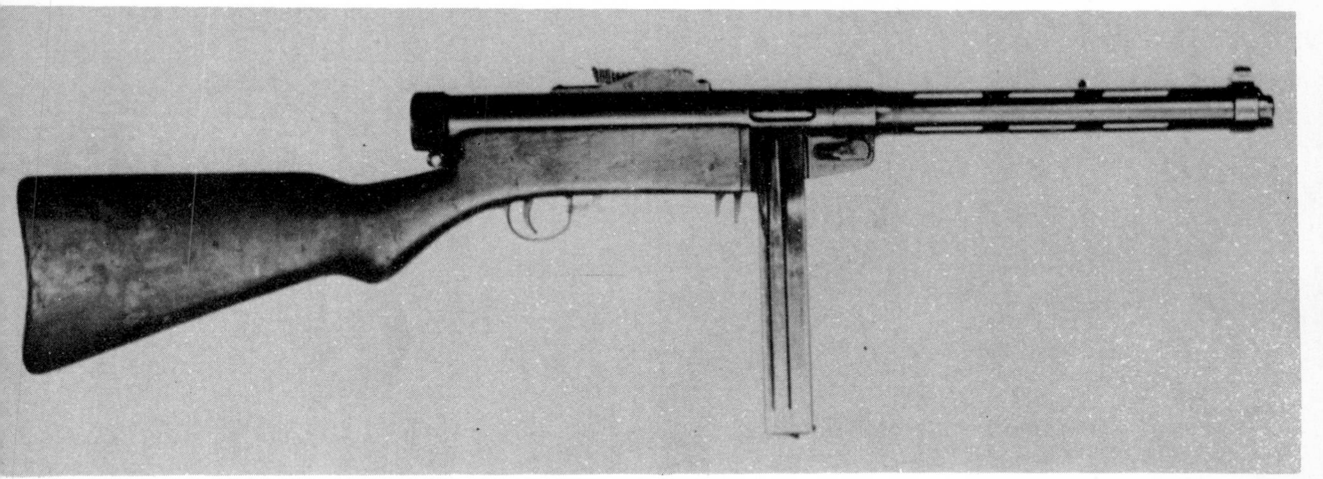

'Suomi' with box magazine

Finnish soldier in action with 'Soumi'

FRANCE

Pistolet Mitrailleur Type SE-M.A.S. 1935F
Mitraillette M.A.S. modèle 38

DATA (modèle 38)
CALIBRE 7.65 mm 0.301 in
LENGTH 623 mm 24.9 in
LENGTH OF BARREL 224 mm 8.8 in
WEIGHT 2.871 kg 6.38 lb
M.V. 350 m/s 1150 ft/sec
CYCLIC RATE OF FIRE 600-700 rpm
MAGAZINE CAPACITY 32 rounds

Development of a sub-machine gun to arm the French forces was slow and steady but by 1935 the first example to be offered for service use was the SE-M.A.S. I almost every respect it was identical to the later M.A.S. modèle 38, but the SE-M.A.S. had a metal 'skeleton' butt. This metal butt was replaced by a conventiona wooden butt on the M.A.S.38, and the French Army then had one of the bes sub-machine gun designs in use prior to 1939. The SE-M.A.S. was put into service i small numbers but the main production version was the M.A.S. modèle 38. This wa a 'straight-line' design with the receiver at a slight angle to the butt, and a conventional blow-back operation. Most parts were extensively machined and the overal design was light and easy to use. The main drawback of the design was that it was chambered for the French 7.65 mm long pistol round which lacked striking powe and range, and had the added export disadvantage that no other nation used the round. Production was carried out at Saint-Etienne and was only just getting unde way when the German invasion of May 1940 took place, but the plant was kept ir limited production to provide weapons for French police units working for the Germans and even for German occupation units. Some were also used by Vichy French forces. German designation was 7.65 mm MP 722(f) for both types. Free French forces also used both types.

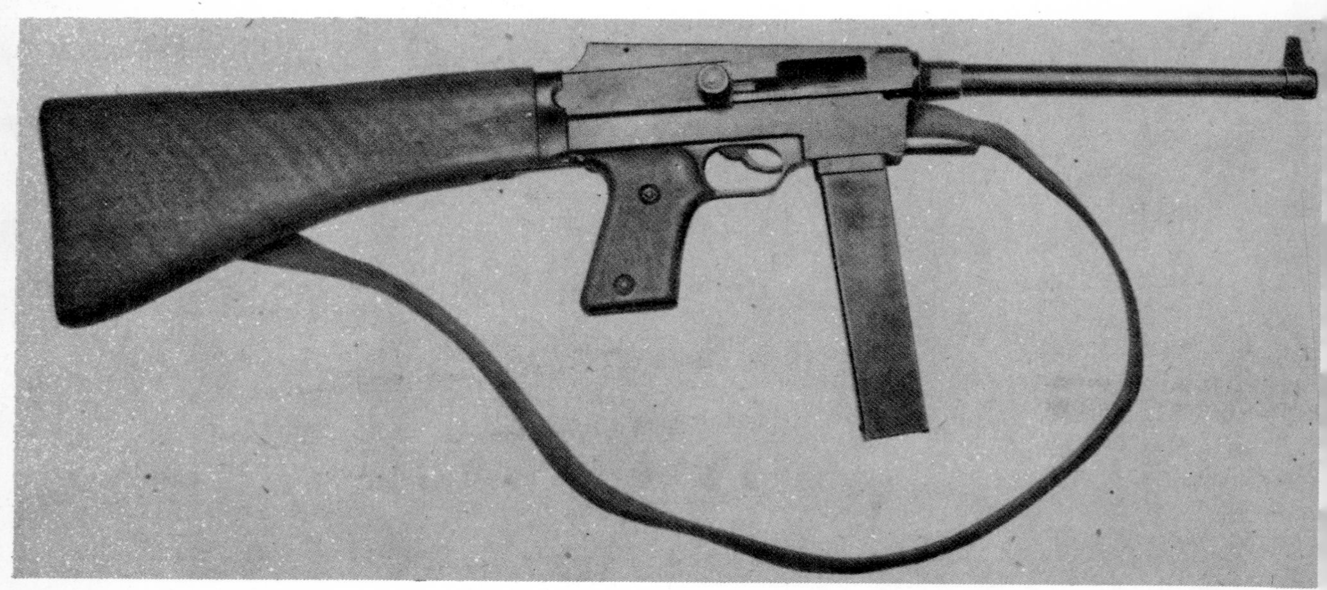

Mitrailette M.A.S.modele 38

MAS modele 38 with 32 round magazine

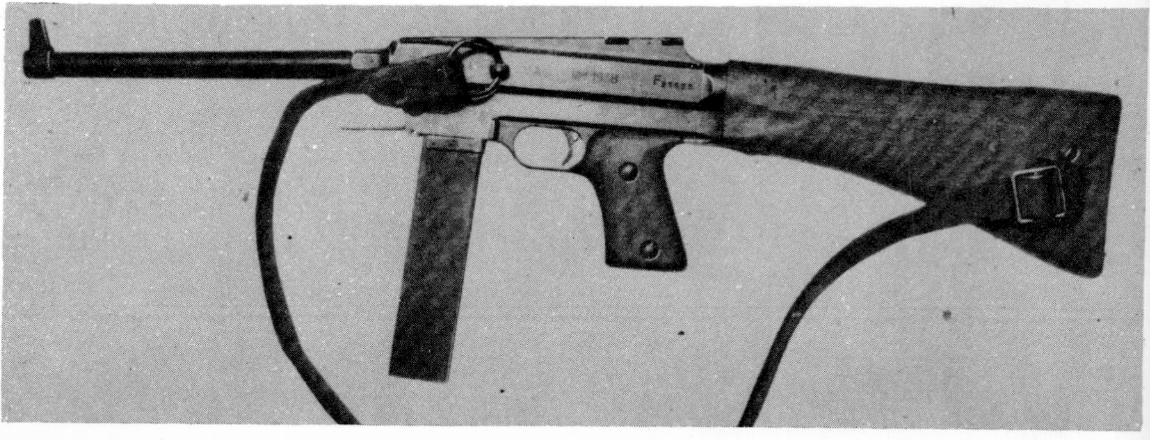

Pistolet Mitrailleur Type E.T.V.S.

DATA
CALIBRE 7.65 mm 0.301 in
LENGTH–BUTT EXTENDED 670 mm 26.38 in
LENGTH–BUTT FOLDED 420 mm 16.53 in
LENGTH OF BARREL 210 mm 8.27 in
WEIGHT 2.7 kg 5.95 lb
M.V. 350 m/s 1150 ft/sec
CYCLIC RATE OF FIRE 500 rpm
MAGAZINE CAPACITY 32 rounds

Although it was not produced in very large numbers the Type E.T.V.S. was in small-scale service with the French forces in 1940 as it appears in lists of captured equipment dated 1941, and indeed the Germans went so far as to allot it an 'own-use' designation (MP 721(f)). The Type E.T.V.S. was a conventional weapon for its time but had the odd distinction of being one of the very first sub-machine guns to feature a folding butt. The Type E.T.V.S. had a hinge on the left side of the small of the butt and the whole butt could be hinged forward for ease when carrying. The service acceptance of the M.A.S. modèle 38 prevented any full scale production of the Type E.T.V.S.

Fusil Mitrailleur RSC modèle 1918

The first production version of the RSC modèle 1918 was the modèle 1917 issued in that year. The modèle 1917 was not a very great success as a self-loading rifle as it was heavy and unreliable. The later modèle 1918 which was intended to correct these faults was little better and due to production delays it was not issued for service until after the Great War had finished. After 1918 the modèle 1918, often known as the 'St. Etienne', was kept in use but its general unreliability meant it was usually issued to colonial or reserve forces and during 1935 a programme was begun to convert them to conventional bolt action rifles. This programme was not fully completed for in 1940 the German forces took numbers into their armoury for use in Russia during 1941 and 1942 as the 8 mm Selbstlade-Gewehr 310(f), such was their need for weapons. After 1942 they appear to have been issued to occupation units in France and the type was also used by the Vichy French in North Africa. Perhaps the most remarkable thing about the modèle 1918 is that it survived so long.

DATA
CALIBRE 8 mm 0.315 in
LENGTH 1120 mm 44.1 in
LENGTH OF BARREL 587 mm 23.1 in
WEIGHT 4.78 kg 10.5 lb
M.V. 665 m/s 2180 ft/sec
MAGAZINE CAPACITY 5 rounds

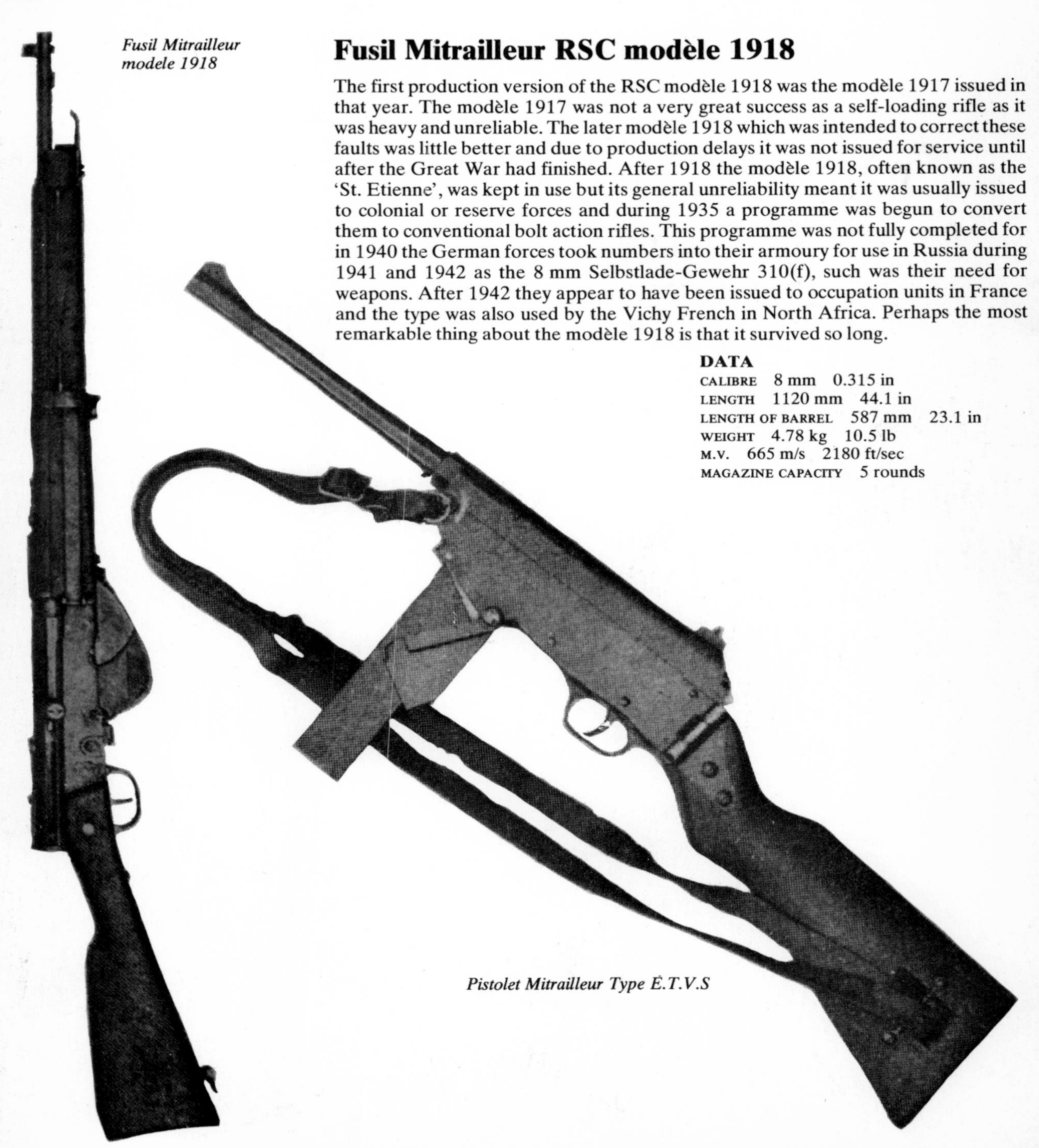

Fusil Mitrailleur modele 1918

Pistolet Mitrailleur Type E.T.V.S

Above: French Portable Flame Thrower P.4. Compressed air cylinder is on the left of the fuel tank. Below: Close-up of flame gun showing the lever type trigger. Range 10-12m; 8 litres; duration of fire, 5 minutes

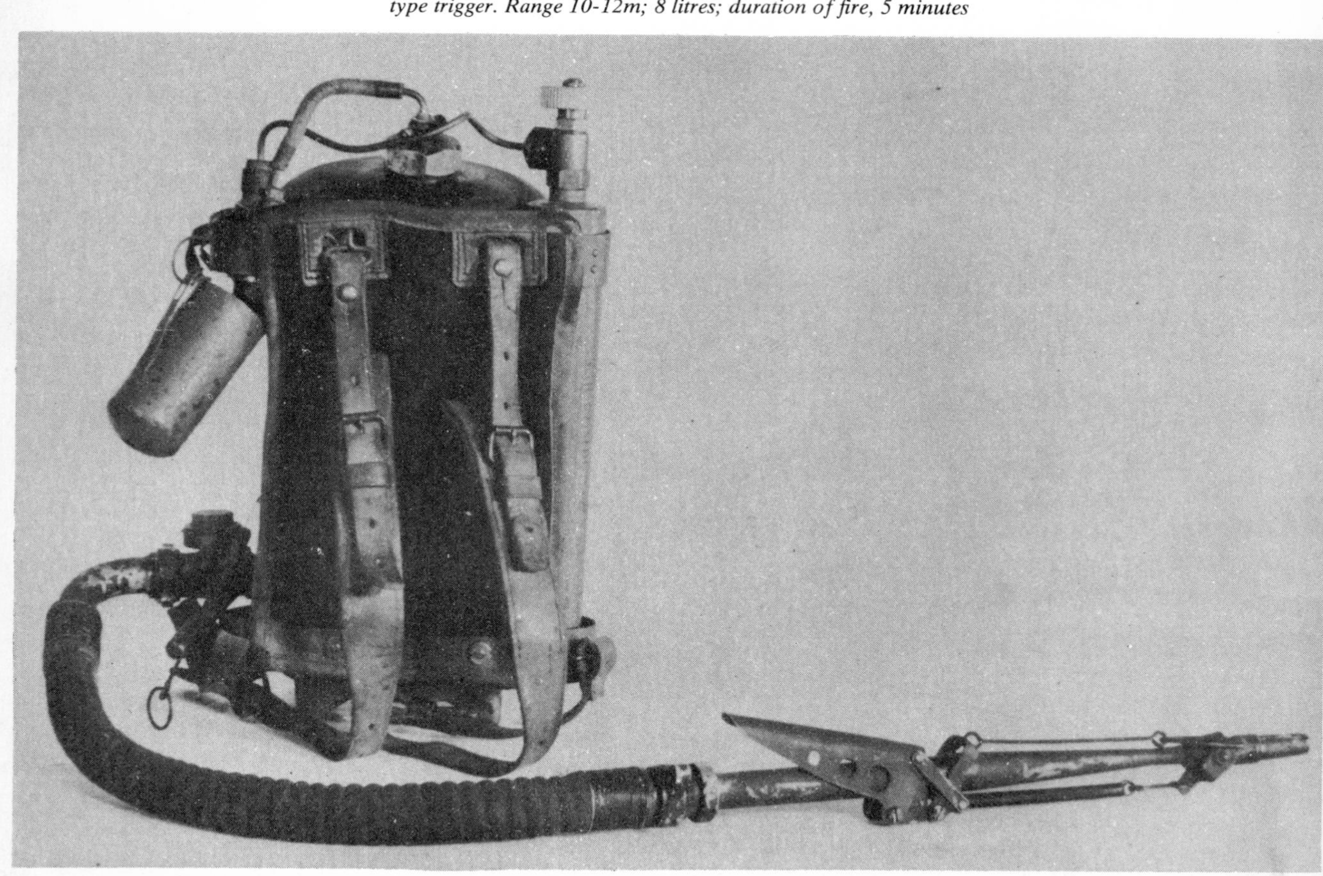

GERMANY

Maschinenpistole 18/1

The MP18/1 was the first German sub-machine gun to be adopted by the German Army and the first examples were issued just before the Great War ended in 1918. These early examples all used a 'snail' magazine. After 1918 a number were issued to the German civil police and during the early 1920s most of these were modified to take a box-type magazine. Manufacture of the MP18/1 in its modified form was continued in Switzerland during the 1920s by SIG and a few were made in Belgium by Pieper. The Swiss versions were made in a variety of calibres for export all over the world, and many were bought by South American states and China. One version, the Type BE, was bought by Japan in 7.63 mm Mauser calibre.

After 1939 many MP18/1 guns were taken into Wehrmacht use for issue to second-line units.

ATA
ALIBRE 9 mm 0.354 in
ENGTH 815 mm 32.1 mm
ENGTH OF BARREL 200 mm 7.88 in
EIGHT 4.177 kg 9.2 lb
.V. 381 m/s 1250 ft/sec
YCLIC RATE OF FIRE 400 rpm
AGAZINE CAPACITY 32 rounds

Maschinenpistole 18/1

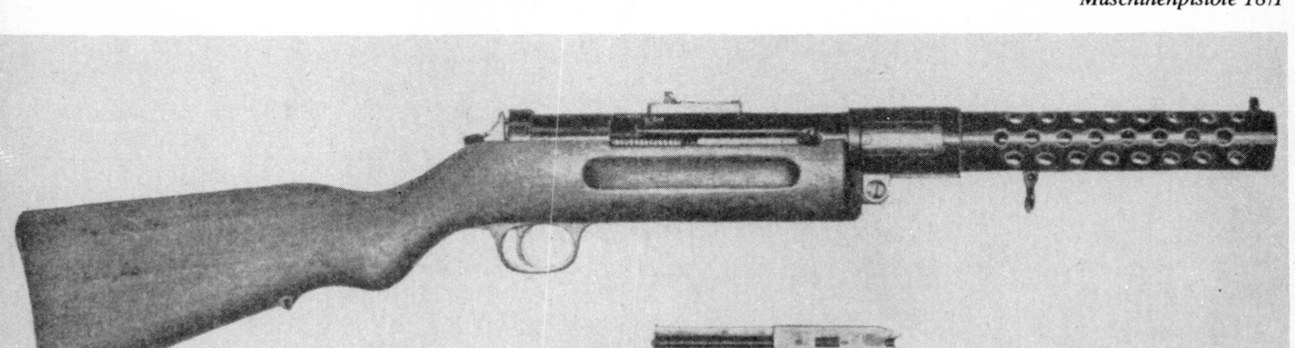

Maschinenpistole 28/11

The M28/11 was basically a modified MP18/1 and differed mainly in having a fire selector mechanism (single or automatic) in place of the automatic-only capacity of the MP 8/1. There were a few internal changes also, but the MP28/11 was intended as a commercial venture for export only, and as a result there were versions in several calibres with small modifications to suit individual customers, but most were delivered in 9 mm Parabellum. Many were sold to China, Japan and many South American states, and in Europe the MP28/11 was sold to Belgium. The type was made in Belgium by Anciens Establishments Pieper at Herstal for the Belgian Army as the Mitrailette 34, and indeed many of the export models of the MP28/11 were made at Herstal under licence from the German Haenel concern. The MP28/11 was widely used during the Spanish Civil War and after 1939 and 1940 the type was used extensively by various German service arms. Many entered German use after the Belgian surrender of 1940 – these were officially the MP 740(b), but do not appear to have been referred to as anything else than the MP28/11.

DATA
ALIBRE 9 mm 0.354 in
ENGTH 813 mm 32 in
ENGTH OF BARREL 200 mm 7.88 in
VEIGHT 4 kg 8.8 lb
M.V. 381 m/s 1250 ft/sec
YCLIC RATE OF FIRE 500 rpm
MAGAZINE CAPACITY 20, 32 or 50 rounds

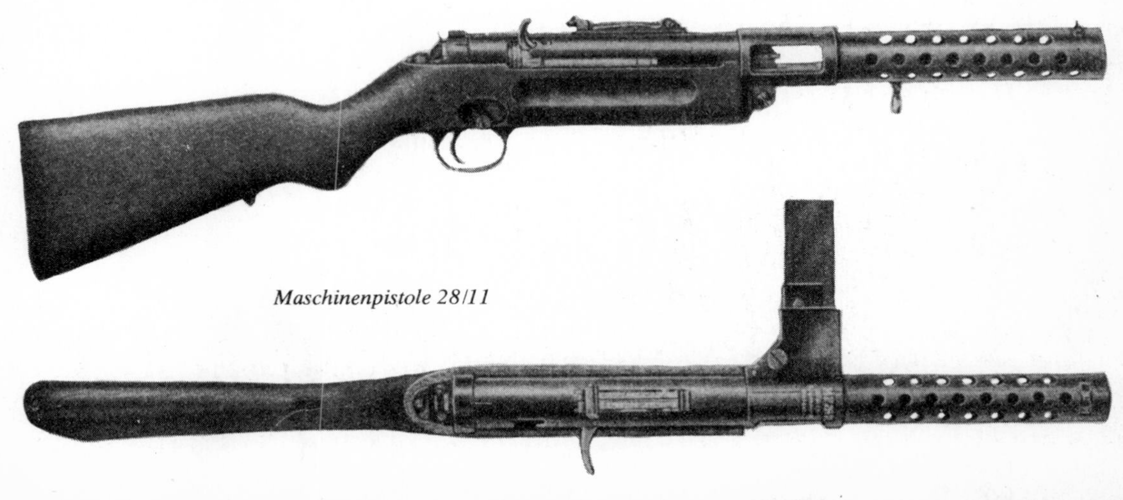

Maschinenpistole 28/11

M.P. 28/11 in action with Finnish soldier on Petsamo Front 1940

Maschinenpistole 34/1
Maschinenpistole 35/1

The sub-machine gun that was designed by Theodor Bergmann and was to become the MP34/1 was first produced in Denmark in 1932. This version, the Bergmann Maschinen-Karabiner Modell 1932 (BMK 32), was made by Schultz-Larsen Gevärfabrik at Otterup, and a small number were made for the Danish Army. In 1934 production started in Germany of the MP34/1 which was produced for export in a number of calibres, but the main production model was the MP35/1 produced for the Waffen SS by Junker und Ruh AG at Karlsruhe. The MP35/1 (usually referred to as the MP35) followed the usual Bergmann design layout but could be identified by the magazine which protruded to the right, instead of the more usual left. The trigger mechanism of the MP35/1 was unusual in that partial pulling produced single shots and automatic fire was produced when the trigger was pulled right back. About 40,000 had been made by the time production ended in 1945 and the entire output was delivered to the SS.

The MP34/1 was produced for such countries as Ethiopia, and the type was also adopted for Danish Army use. A small batch was delivered to the German Police, but total production did not exceed 2,000.

DATA (MP34/1)
CALIBRE 9 mm 0.354 in
LENGTH 955 mm 37.6 in
LENGTH OF BARREL 320 mm 12.6 in
WEIGHT 4.04 kg 8.9 lb
M.V. 381 m/s 1250 ft/sec
CYCLIC RATE OF FIRE 650 rpm
MAGAZINE CAPACITY 32 rounds

Maschinenpistole 35/1

Opposite: German soldier armed with the M.P 35/1

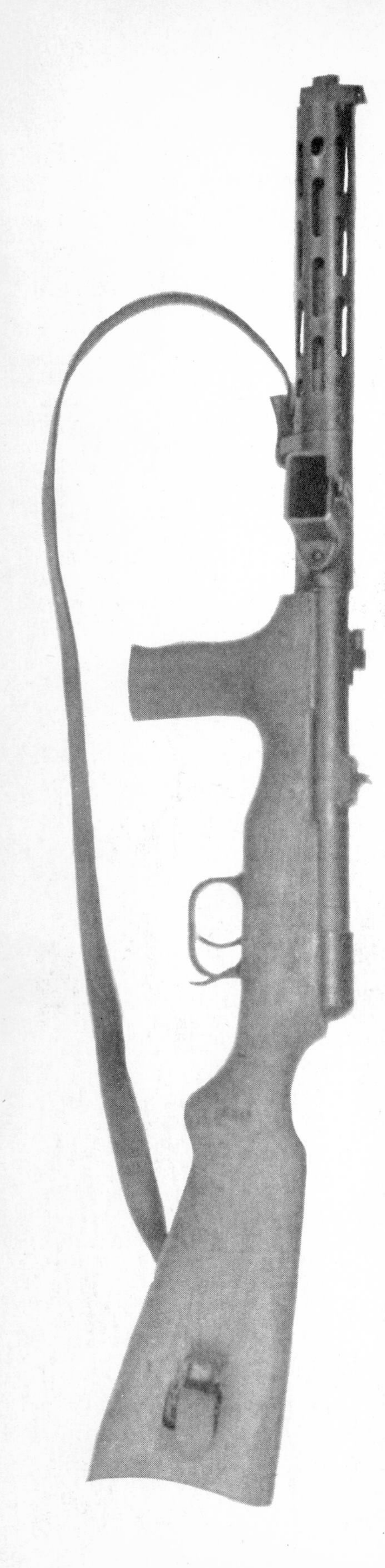

Maschinenpistole Erma

The MP Erma was developed from the earlier Vollmer machine pistol designe during the 1920s. The design had been taken over by the Erma-Werke in time for production order to partly equip the expanding German forces where it remained first-line weapon until about 1942 when it was gradually phased to second-line ar reserve units. The main feature of the MP Erma (or MPE) was the mainspri contained in a telescopic housing which effectively kept out dust and dirt, and th manufacturing process which used steel tubing where possible to keep down ma ufacturing costs. The main identification point of the MP Erma was the vertic foregrip (although some had a conventional straight horizontal foregrip).

Some MP Erma sub-machine guns were exported to France (Pistolet mitraille Vollmer Erma), and a small batch were sold to Jugoslavia – these had longer barre than the 'standard' model. The MP Erma was also produced in Spain.

A variant of the basic Erma design was a silenced version which was produced small numbers and issued to French Security police operating under German gu dance.

DATA Standard MP Erma
CALIBRE 9 mm 0.354 in
LENGTH 902 mm 35.5 in
LENGTH OF BARREL 251 mm 9.9 in
WEIGHT 4.154 kg 9.2 lb
M.V. 381 m/s 1250 ft/sec
CYCLIC RATE OF FIRE 500 rpm
MAGAZINE CAPACITY 20 or 32 rounds

Silenced version
CALIBRE 9 mm 0.354 in
LENGTH 1187.5 mm 46.75 in
LENGTH OF BARREL 248.5 mm 9.785 in
WEIGHT 4.74 kg 10.45 lb
M.V. (approx) 305 m/s 1000 ft/sec
CYCLIC RATE OF FIRE 350 rpm
MAGAZINE CAPACITY 32 rounds

Left: Maschinenpistole Erma. Below: German troops with Maschinenpistole Erma, in action on Russian front

Maschinenpistole 38
Maschinenpistole 38/40

DATA
CALIBRE 9 mm 0.354 in
LENGTH – STOCK EXTENDED 833 mm 32.8 in
LENGTH – STOCK FOLDED 630 mm 24.8 in
LENGTH OF BARREL 251.5 mm 9.9 in
WEIGHT 4.086 kg 9 lb
M.V. 381 m/s 1250 ft/sec
CYCLIC RATE OF FIRE 500 rpm
MAGAZINE CAPACITY 32 rounds

The MP 38 was the forebear of the MP40 and with it it has become one of the most famous of all sub-machine guns. The MP38 was a product of the Erma-Werke at Erfurt and when it first appeared it embodied many novel features. The mainspring was contained in a telescopic sleeve, as used on the MP Erma, but it also had a folding metal butt and no wood was used in its construction. Only steel and plastics were used. The MP38 was designed from the start with the needs of airborne and mobile troops in mind, and thus had the folding butt and the magazine pointing vertically downwards. The MP38 was in production from 1938 until 1940 when its place on the production lines was taken by the MP40.

In service the MP38 was very well received but battle experience in Poland showed the need for some form of safety on the cocking handle when in the forward position. The original cocking handle on the MP38 was a one-piece handle and if it was jarred or knocked when a round was in the chamber, the round could be fired. A simple modification was embodied to prevent this happening by having a folding latch on the cocking handle which engaged in a notch on the receiver when forward, thus preventing any bolt movement. With this change embodied the MP38 was redesignated the MP38/40, and the change was gradually fitted to most MP38s after 1940.

The MP38 was known to the Allies as the 'Schmeisser' but no reason for this title can be found as Hugo Schmeisser had no hand in its design. Like the MP40 the MP38 became a sought-after trophy by the Allies and large numbers found their way into the hands of various resistance and partisan forces. Together with the MP40 the MP38 was used as front-line equipment by the Russian Army and the MP38 was one of the more important weapons used by the Jugoslav partisans.

Maschinenpistole 38 in service with Russian Ski Troops

DATA (MP40)
As MP38 except:
WEIGHT 4.027 kg 8.87 lb
MP40/11
As MP38 except:
WEIGHT 4.54 kg 10 lb
MAGAZINE CAPACITY 2 × 32 rounds

Maschinenpistole 40
Maschinenpistole 40/11

While the MP38 was an undoubted success, it proved to be rather expensive and time-consuming to manufacture. A major redesign was carried out on the MP38 which resulted in an almost identical weapon which was far more suited to the production needs of modern war. Machining processes were cut to a minimum and steel pressings and welds were used wherever possible. With these changes the new design became the MP40 and it was mass produced in a number of German centres. Extensive use was made of sub-contractors to make sub-assemblies. The MP40 set an example for quick and cheap production that has been followed ever since and this has made it one of the most important sub-machine gun designs of the Second World War. Although it was first issued to special-purpose and front-line units its use spread to all arms of the German forces and the MP40 became one of the most prized of Allied war trophies. There were numerous examples of the MP40 being preferred to Allied equivalents, and the Red Army used as many as it could capture as a front-line weapon.

Experience on the Russian Front revealed that the MP40 was sometimes at a tactical disadvantage when opposed by the Russian PPSh fitted with a 71-round drum magazine (the MP40 magazine held only 32 rounds). In an attempt to provide more readily-available ammunition the MP40/11 was devised. This used a rather clumsy device which held two MP40 magazines side-by-side. As one magazine was emptied the other could be quickly moved over to enable firing to continue. The MP40/11 was first issued in 1943 but it was not a great success and few appear to have been made.

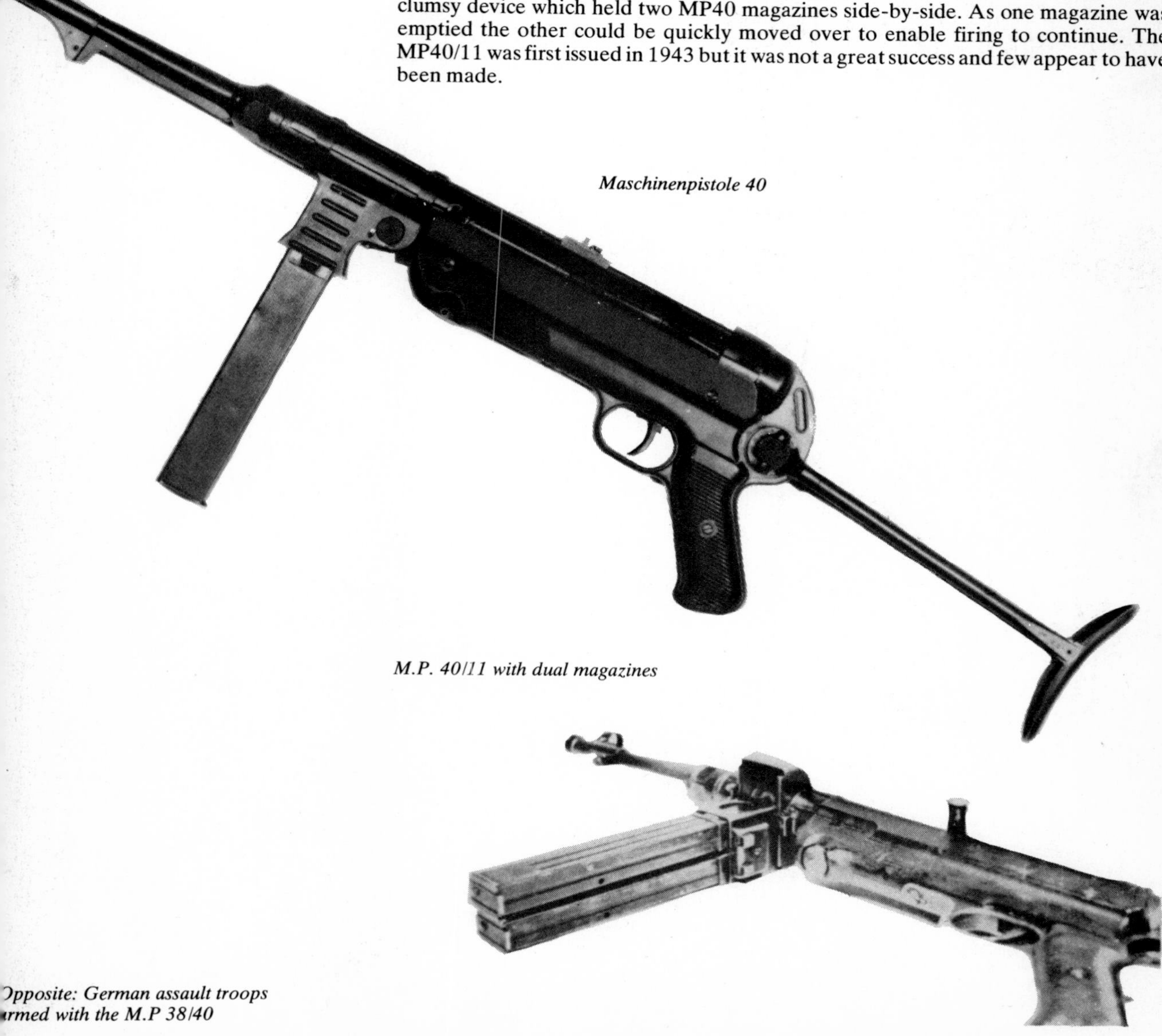

Maschinenpistole 40

M.P. 40/11 with dual magazines

Opposite: German assault troops armed with the M.P 38/40

Side view of M.P. 40/11 with twin magazines

Maschinenpistole 41

Despite the trend set by the MP38 and 40 with their all-metal construction and ease of production, the MP41 was a throw-back to earlier days. It was produced by Haenel from a Schmeisser development of the MP40 design as it used the same barrel and bolt as the MP40 fitted to a wooden stock similar to that used on the MP28/11. Small numbers of the MP41 were manufactured but their eventual destination is uncertain as the type was not adopted by the German forces or police. It is thus possible that they were delivered to a force under German control in one of the occupied territories.

DATA
CALIBRE 9 mm 0.354 in
LENGTH 863.5 mm 34 in
LENGTH OF BARREL 251.5 mm 9.9 in
WEIGHT 3.7 kg 8.15 lb
M.V. 381 m/s 1250 ft/sec
CYCLIC RATE OF FIRE 500 rpm
MAGAZINE CAPACITY 32 rounds

Maschinenpistole 41

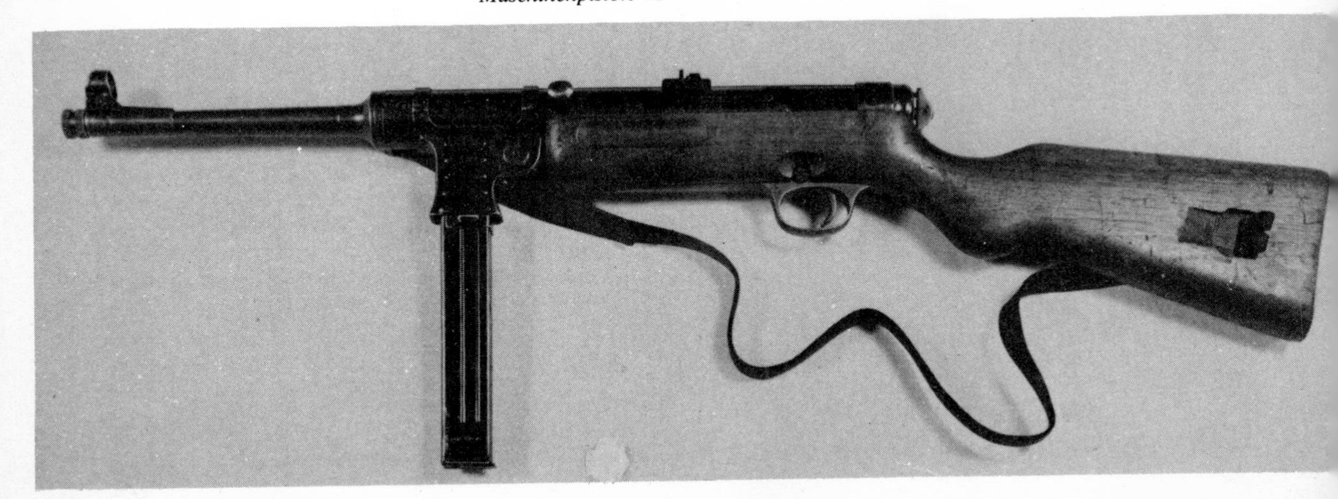

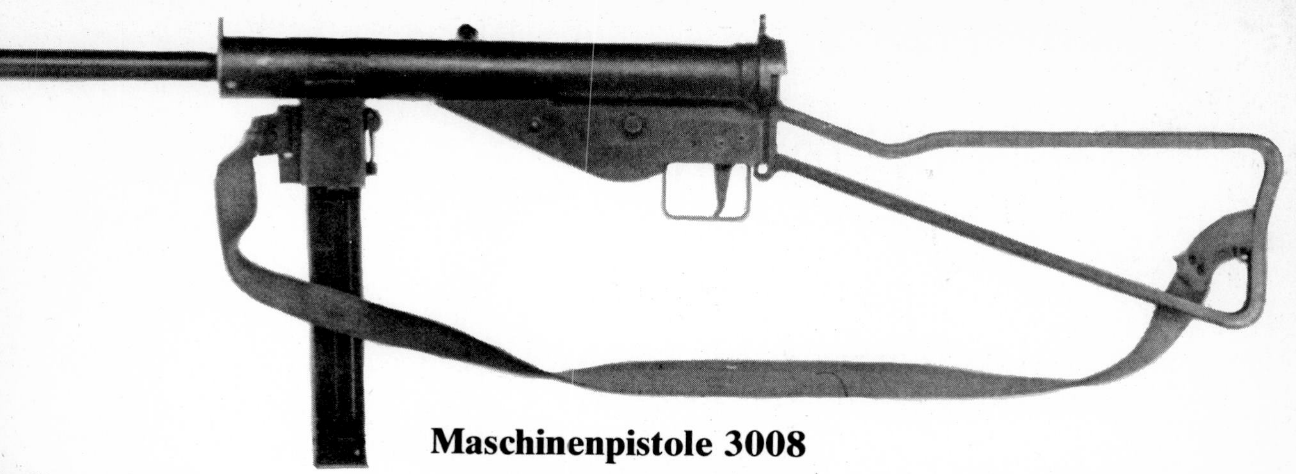

ɫaschinenpistole 3008, ˈerman copy of ritish Sten

Maschinenpistole 3008

As the winter of 1944 started the German forces were forced back along all fronts and their manufacturing facilities were either falling into enemy hands or were being pounded to rubble by Allied bombers. Huge amounts of war material and weapons had been and were being lost and the need to equip the remaining fighting units continued. In an attempt to provide some form of weapon for the infantry and Volksturm the German planners decided to use the British Sten Gun as a starting point for a sub-machine gun design. The Sten had proved easy and simple to make and so the design was virtually copied direct with the one real change being made to the magazine housing which was produced pointing vertically downwards with no facility to rotate. There were many variations on the basic design with changes being effected to suit the particular factory that was producing the weapon. The designation of the Sten-derived weapon was MP3008, and by the time the war ended about 10,000 had been produced. How many of these saw action is uncertain but some were used in battle and several examples were captured by Allied forces before May 1945. The standard of manufacture of the MP3008 was very low and their life in battle would have been very short, but they worked.

DATA
CALIBRE 9 mm 0.354 in
LENGTH 795 mm 31.3 in
LENGTH OF BARREL 198 mm 7.8 in
WEIGHT 2.95 kg 6.5 lb
M.V. 381 m/s 1250 ft/sec
CYCLIC RATE OF FIRE 500 rpm
MAGAZINE CAPACITY 32 rounds

7.92 mm Gewehr 41(W)
7.92 mm Gewehr 41(M)

By 1940 the Wehrmacht tactical study groups finally issued a specification for a self-loading rifle and both Walther and Mauser put forward almost identical design studies. Prototypes of both rifles were made and issued for troop trials where the Mauser design, the Gew 41(M), soon showed itself to be unsuitable for service use and was thus withdrawn. The Walther design used an almost identical gas-operated mechanism to the Mauser rifle as it used a slight variation of the Danish Bang system. The Bang system trapped muzzle gases and diverted them to the rear to operate a piston which in turn operated the ejection/loading mechanism. The Gew 41(W) was put into production but it was not a great success. It was difficult to manufacture and in the field it soon proved difficult to load quickly and was prone to be rather unreliable due to the complex mechanism. Also it was heavy for its role and generally 'unhandy'. Most of these rifles, usually referred to as the Gew 41, went to the Russian Front and were rarely encountered elsewhere. Production ceased as soon as the Gew 43 entered production, but the Gew 41 remained in use until 1945.

DATA (Gew 41(W))
CALIBRE 7.92 mm 0.312 in
LENGTH 1124 mm 44.25 in
LENGTH OF BARREL 546 mm 21.5 in
WEIGHT 5.03 kg 11.08 lb
M.V. 776 m/s 2250 ft/sec
MAGAZINE CAPACITY 10 rounds

(Gew 41(M))
CALIBRE 7.92 mm 0.312 in
LENGTH 1175 mm 46.25 in
LENGTH OF BARREL 552.5 mm 21.75 in
WEIGHT 5.1 kg 11.25 lb
M.V. 776 m/s 2250 ft/sec
MAGAZINE CAPACITY 10 rounds

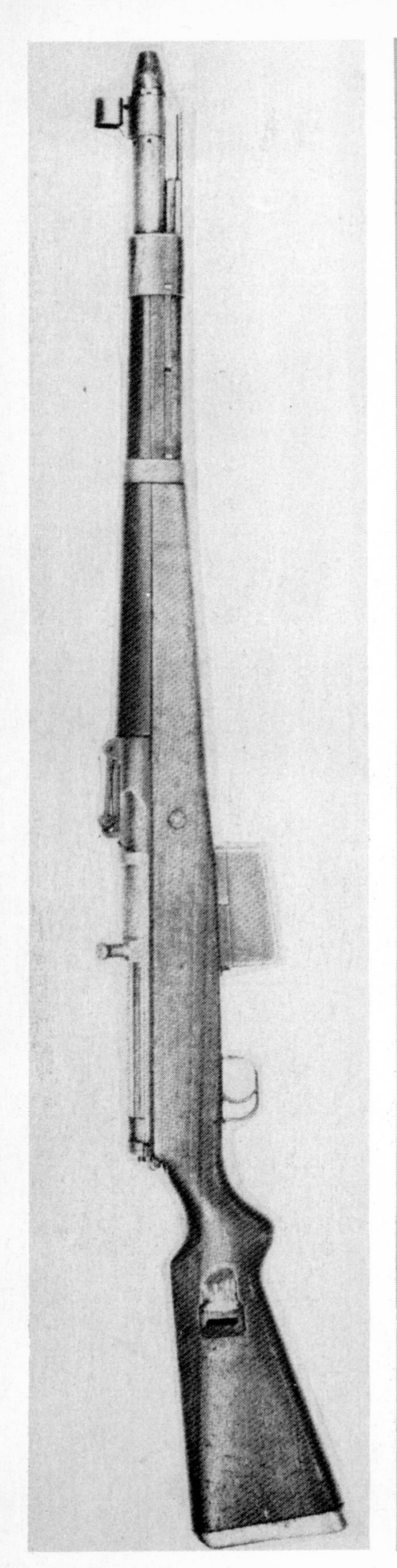

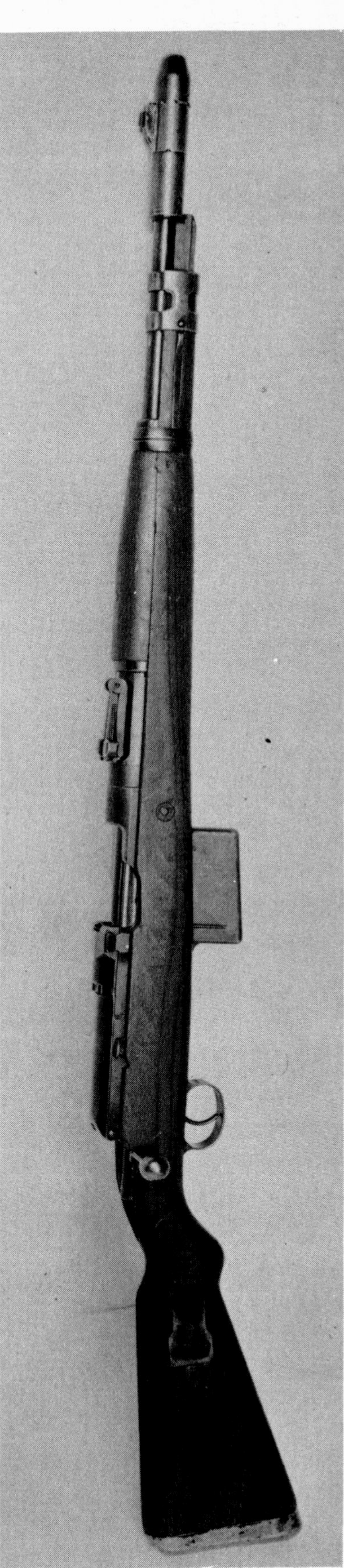

Left: 7.92 mm Gewehr 41 (W)
Right: 7.92 mm Gewehr 41 (M)

7.92 mm Gewehr 43
7.92 mm Karabiner 43

7.92 mm Gewehr 43

As large numbers of Russian Tokarev semi-automatic rifles fell into German hands during 1941 and 1942 it was seen that the Russian gas-operated mechanism had many advantages over the system used on the Gew 41. Thus the Gew 41 was altered so that the original Walther bolt mechanism was actuated by a gas system very similar to the Russian original. The result was the Gew 43 which like the earlier Gew 41 fired the normal 7.92 mm cartridge. The Gew 43 was produced in large numbers and was a much more viable and reliable weapon than the earlier Gew 41. It was much easier to produce, and incorporated such features as laminated wooden furniture, simple forgings and a minimum of machined parts. Loading was eased by making the magazine detachable when it could be loaded from two five-round clips. A bracket for a Zf41 telescopic sight was standard. The Kar 43 was only about 2 in (51 mm) shorter than the Gew 43, and seems to have been introduced into service with several manufacturing modifications some time in 1944. The Gew 43 and Kar 43 were made in large numbers and remained in production until the war ended.

DATA (Gew 43)
CALIBRE 7.92 mm 0.312 in
LENGTH 1117 mm 44 in
LENGTH OF BARREL 549 mm 21.62 in
WEIGHT 4.4 kg 9.56 lb
M.V. (approx) 776 m/s 2550 ft/sec
MAGAZINE CAPACITY 10 rounds

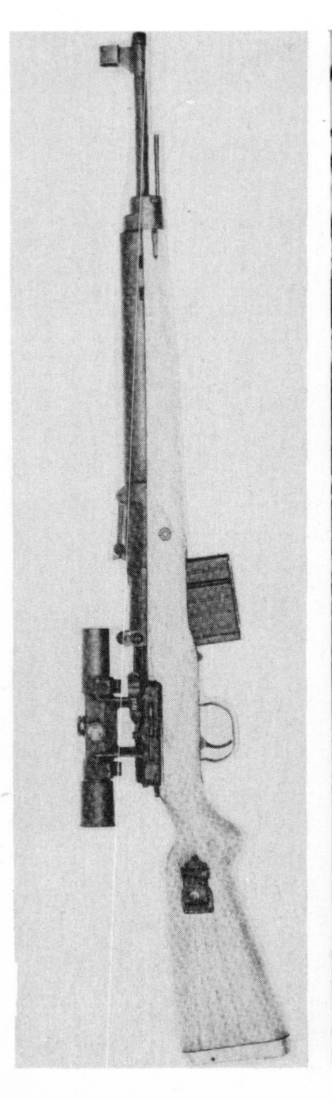

7.92mm Karabiner 43 with Zf 41 telescopic sight

German infantrymen armed with the Karabiner 43

7.92 mm Fallschirmjägergewehr 42

The German paratroop arm came under Luftwaffe control and thus supply of their weapons was separate from that of the Wehrmacht. When Wehrmacht specifications for assault rifles were made the Luftwaffe decided not to adopt the 7.92 mm kurz round but instead retained the standard round and asked Rheinmetall to design a new automatic weapon suitable for paratroop use. The result, the FG 42, was one of the more remarkable designs to emerge from World War 2. None of the mechanism detail was entirely new, but when assembled together the result was a reliable compact weapon that could be used to fire a normal cartridge as an assault rifle. In many ways the FG 42 resembled a light machine gun and it even had a light bipod permanently fixed. But it also had a fixed folding bayonet and the barrel could not be easily changed. There were two main versions which differed only in that one version had a steel butt and a sloping pistol grip while the other had a wooden butt and conventional grip. The mechanism was gas-operated and was widely copied for other designs after the war as it fired from a closed bolt for semi-automatic fire and from an open bolt for automatic fire. For all its design advantages the FG 42 was not an easy or cheap design to produce and only about 7,000 were made.

DATA
CALIBRE 7.92 mm 0.312 in
LENGTH 940 mm 37 in
LENGTH OF BARREL 502 mm 19.75 in
WEIGHT 4.53 kg 9.94 lb
M.V. 761 m/s 2500 ft/sec
CYCLIC RATE OF FIRE 750-800 rpm
MAGAZINE CAPACITY 20 rounds

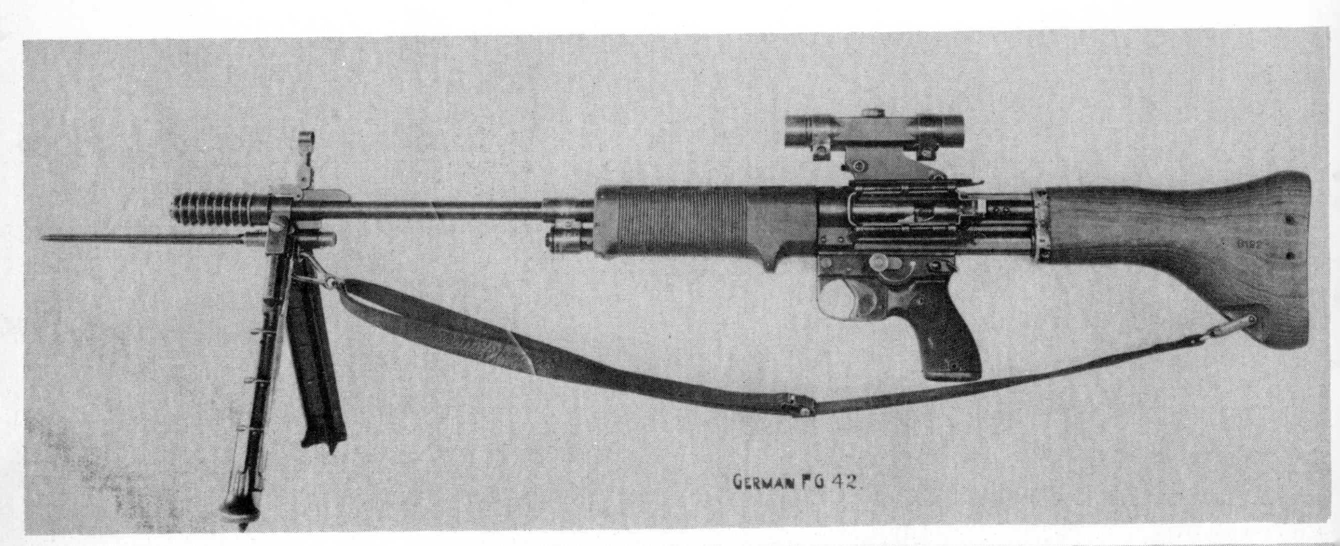

7.92 mm Fallschirmjägergewehr 42 with wooden butt, equipped with Zf 42 scope

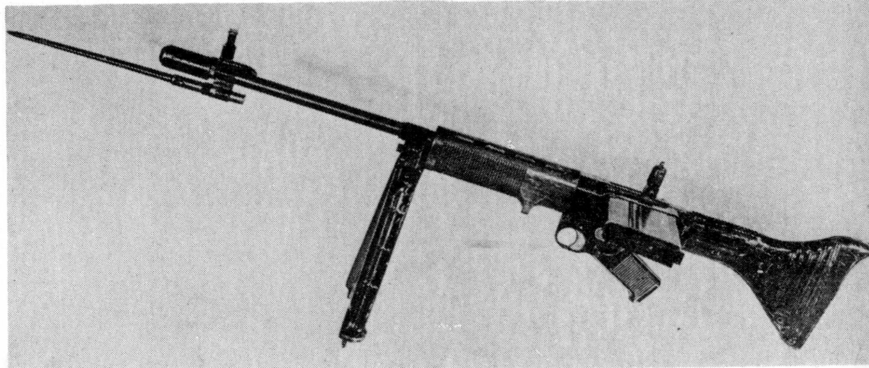

7.92 mm Fallschirmjägergewehr 42 with metal butt

German airman demonstrates the F.G 42 without the aid of the bipod. Note that the bayonet is folded

Maschinenkarabiner 42(H)

From 1939 onwards the German Army kept detailed combat reports which were continually analysed for tactical trends, new equipment requirements, etc. One lesson that emerged was that the standard rifle cartridge was unnecessarily powerful as most shooting was done at ranges of less than 400 metres. A less powerful round could thus be used, with the result that the weapon firing this reduced power round could be lighter, handier and incorporate an automatic fire capacity. A new cartridge that emerged from a series of trials was a short 7.92 mm round known as the 7.92 mm kurz or intermediate round. New rifle designs were submitted by Walther and Haenel, and of the two the Haenel design was the most successful. The Haenel submission was designed by Louis Schmeisser and emerged as a gas-operated weapon with several features designed to ease manufacture. It was known to the Wehrmacht as the MKb42(H), and about 8,000 were produced for troop trials on the Eastern Front where it soon proved very successful. These early models were usually issued to elite units, and the bulk of production was carried out in the remarkable time of three months. Combat experience with the MKb42(H) led to some changes being made to produce the MP43.

DATA
CALIBRE 7.92 mm 0.312 in
LENGTH 940 mm 37 in
LENGTH OF BARREL 364 mm 14.37 in
WEIGHT 4.9 kg 10.81 lb
M.V. (approx) 640 m/s 2100 ft/sec
CYCLIC RATE OF FIRE 500 rpm
MAGAZINE CAPACITY 30 rounds

Maschinenkarabiner 42 (H)

Maschinenkarabiner 42(W)

The MKb42(W) was designed by Walther Waffenfabrik AG to the same specification that produced the MKb42(H). It used a very similar gas-operated mechanism and followed the same design philosophy as the Haenel design in that it used a large number of simple metal stampings, plastic mouldings and a minimum of machined parts to ease production. Some 3000-5000 were produced during 1942 and were issued for troop trials on the Eastern Front but the Haenel design was selected for mass production and the MKb42(W) was dropped. Those produced remained in use until the end of the war for the simple reason that as many automatic weapons as possible were needed by the troops at the Front.

DATA
CALIBRE 7.92 mm 0.312 in
LENGTH 933.5 mm 36.75 in
LENGTH OF BARREL 409 mm 16.1 in
WEIGHT 4.43 kg 9.75 lb
M.V. 650 m/s 2132 ft/sec
CYCLIC RATE OF FIRE 600 rpm
MAGAZINE CAPACITY 30 rounds

Maschinenkarabiner 42 (W)

DATA

CALIBRE 7.92 mm 0.312 in
LENGTH 940 mm 37 in
LENGTH OF BARREL 419 mm 16.5 in
WEIGHT 5.22 kg 11.5 lb
M.V. 650 m/s 2132 ft/sec
CYCLIC RATE OF FIRE 500 rpm
MAGAZINE CAPACITY 30 rounds

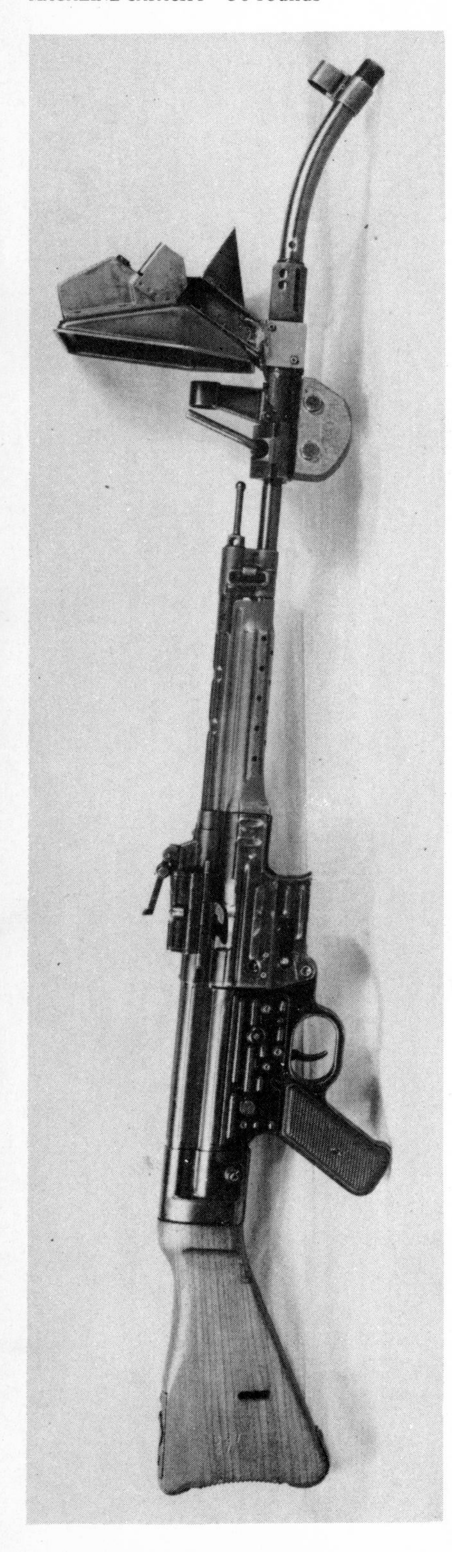

Maschinenpistole 43
Maschinenpistole 43/1
Maschinenpistole 44
Sturmgewehr 44

Experience with the Haenel MKb42(H) produced changes that changed the designation to MP43. The first examples were produced in 1943 and the MP43 remained in production virtually unchanged until the war ended in 1945. Despite the design being produced for ease of production some gradual changes to ease assembly still further were incorporated but the basic design remained unchanged to the end. The MP43/1 was introduced in late 1943, but the only change was the facility to fit a grenade launcher cup to the muzzle – a fitting that seems to have been little used. During 1944 the design designation was changed to MP44 but there were no external changes and eventually the designation was further changed in late 1944 to StG44 (Sturmgewehr 44) apparently for purely political reasons. The MP43 series were very successful weapons that in many ways showed the way that future small arms development was to follow, and they can be regarded as the first true 'assault rifles'. A range of accessories was developed for the MP43 series. One of the most futuristic of these developments was the Zielgerät 1229 'Vampir' infra-red night sight, produced and issued in small numbers in early 1945. Some MP43s were fitted with the GwZf 4-fach telescopic sight, but perhaps the most bizarre fitting was the Krum - mlauf curved barrel fitting. Research has failed to find a viable and sensible reason for this odd development but some were issued for use on some vehicles where their 30° curved barrels and complicated optical sights could be used to some effect.

Left: M.P 44 with the curved barrel fitting 'Krummlauf' a device to enable the gun to 'fire round corners'

Above: German soldier equipped with M.P 43/1

Below: Maschinenpistole 43

Volksturmgewehr 1-5

By late 1944 weapon production in the Reich was getting to such a state that local arrangements had to be made to ensure some form of weapon supply to the newly-formed Volksturm home defence units. One project to use the 7.92 mm kurz round that actually reached production and service was the VG 1-5, a weapon that was something of a cross between a sub-machine gun and a light assault rifle. The VG 1-5 was designed by the Gustloff-Werke of Suhl and production was carried out by as many factories as possible that could still boast machine tools. Overall finish and manufacturing standards were understandably poor but the VG 1-5 had an unusual locking mechanism. When the bullet was fired some of the muzzle gases were tapped to bear on the face of a piston fixed to the bolt. Thus the bolt was held forward until the bullet left the muzzle in a very simple and effective system of delayed blowback. The number of VG 1-5 weapons produced was probably not very high and very few were actually captured by the Allies. Most of these were semi-automatic only weapons but a few were made with a full automatic facility.

DATA
ALIBRE 7.92 mm 0.312 in
ENGTH 885 mm 34.85 in
ENGTH OF BARREL 378 mm 14.9 in
VEIGHT 4.62 kg 10.18 lb
I.V. (approx) 660 m/s 2163 ft/sec
IAGAZINE CAPACITY 30 rounds

Volksturmgewehr 1-5

GERMAN PORTABLE FLAME-THROWERS

Flammenwerfer 35

(Light Portable Flame-thrower (1935 pattern)

This equipment, with which Germany entered the war, was a slightly modified version of that used in 1918. It remained the standard manpack until 1941 when production of this model ceased.

WEIGHT 35.8 kg 79 lb
FUEL 11.8 litres 2.6 galls
RANGE 25.6-30 metres 28-33 yds
DURATION OF FIRE 10 seconds

Flammenwerfer klein verbessert 40

(Light Portable Flame-thrower, modified) Lifebuoy Type (Model 40)

This equipment superseded the 1935 pattern, the advantages being that it was only 47 lb (21.3 kg) in weight and was a better fit on the operator's back. The fuel content was less than the 1935 pattern, but the range remained unaltered.

Flammenwerfer 41

(Light Portable Flame-thrower (Model 41))

This consisted of two cylinders, one for fuel and the other for compressed nitrogen. The complete apparatus weighed 35 to 40lb. This reduction in weight was gained at the expense of its fuel capacity, which was only one and a half gallons.

Flammenwerfer 41 in action, note operators protective clothing

Flammenwerfer 35

Flammenwerfer klein verbessert 40

Flammenwerfer mit Strahlrohrpatrone 41

(Light Portable Flame-thrower with cartridge ignition (Model 41))

In appearance this model was similar to Model 41, but the gun was slightly shorter and differed in one essential point: the ignition system. In 1942 it was found that the ignition system under the extreme cold conditions of the Russian campaign was unreliable, so a new projector was developed with cartridge ignition. This model remained the standard manpack until the end of the war. The apparatus weighed 40 lb full and had a range of 25 to 35 yds.

Einstoss Flammenwerfer tragbar (Model 46))

(Flame-thrower, portable, parachutists)

As the manpack flame-throwers were operated by Engineer Assault Units, a single-shot close combat weapon for Infantry Assault Groups and Paratroops was developed. This weighed about 6½ lb when loaded and consisted of a cylindrical tube with a pistol grip and trigger mechanism attached to the forward end. The weapon was 23½ in long with a diameter of 2¾ in. It projected a single burst of flame of a ½-second duration to a distance of about 30 yds.

Flammenwerfer mit Strahlrohrpatrone 41

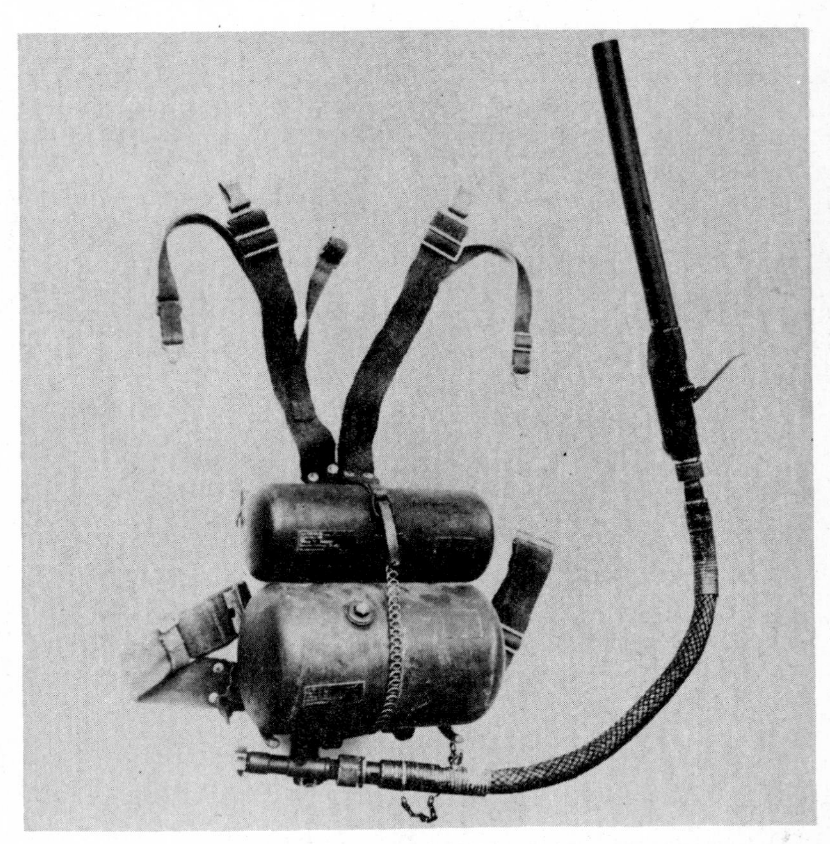

The single-shot flame-thrower

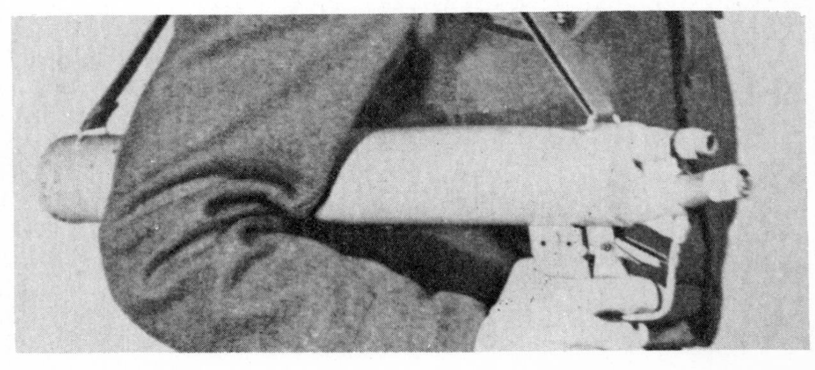

Mittlerer Flammenwerfer (m.Fm.W)

Medium Flame-thrower

WEIGHT 102 kg 224.4 lb
FUEL 29.55 litres 6.5 gall
RANGE 22.9-27.4 metres 25-30 yds
DURATION OF FIRE 25 seconds

Fundamentally this was a trolley-borne version of the 1935 pattern light portable flame-thrower. Mounted on a two-wheeled undercarriage it was pulled by two soldiers with two straps. Though originally issued to Engineer Units in the early days of the war as a field equipment it soon became obsolete and was withdrawn from service. It later reappeared as a static equipment in Coast Defence.

Mittlerer Flammenwerfer

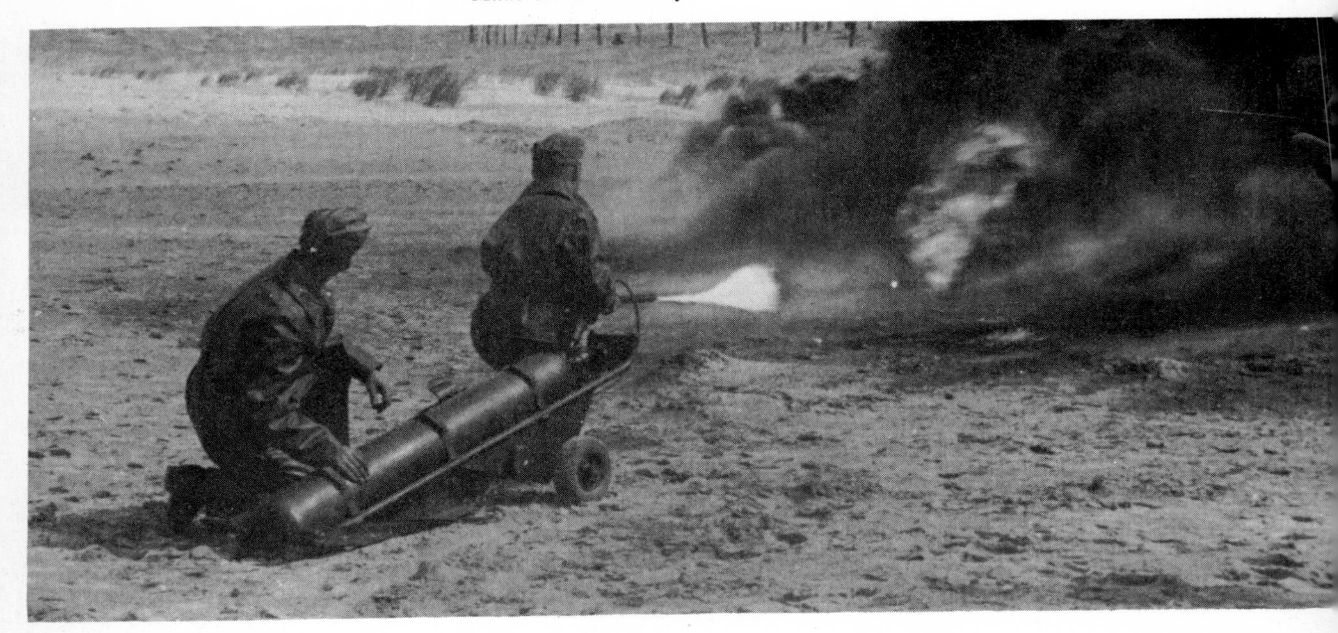

HUNGARY

Gepisztoly 39M
Gepisztoly 43M

Top on opposite page: Gepisztoly 39M

Centre: Gepisztoly 43M

Bottom: 43M model with metal butt and magazine folded

The design of the 39M sub-machine gun has been credited to Pal D. Kiraly who was also responsible for several contemporary designs in the UK and Switzerland. The 39M was adopted for use with the Hungarian Army and was unusual in several respects. It was chambered for the 9 mm Mauser round instead of the usual Parabellum round and it used a two-piece bolt that gave rise to a form of retarded blowback in order to produce a steady weapon when fired. As the 39M was a rather long and heavy sub-machine gun this made it a very accurate weapon to fire and the sights were optimistically calibrated up to 600 metres accordingly. A further unusual point was that the long magazine could be folded forward for carrying. A variant produced in small numbers was the 39M/A which had a folding wooden butt.

The 43M was produced in larger numbers than the 39M and was the same weapon with a folding metal butt and a slightly shorter barrel.

DATA (39M)
CALIBRE 9 mm 0.354 in
LENGTH 1048 mm 41.25 in
LENGTH OF BARREL 499 mm 19.65 in
WEIGHT 3.723 kg 8.2 lb
M.V. 450 m/s 1475 ft/sec
CYCLIC RATE OF FIRE 750 rpm
MAGAZINE CAPACITY 20 or 40 rounds

Data (43M)
CALIBRE 9 mm 0.354 in
LENGTH–BUTT EXTENDED 956 mm 37.5 in
LENGTH–BUTT FOLDED 749 mm 29.5 in
LENGTH OF BARREL 424 mm 16.7 in
WEIGHT 3.63 kg 8 lb
M.V. 442 m/s 1450 ft/sec
CYCLIC RATE OF FIRE 750 rpm
MAGAZINE CAPACITY 40 rounds

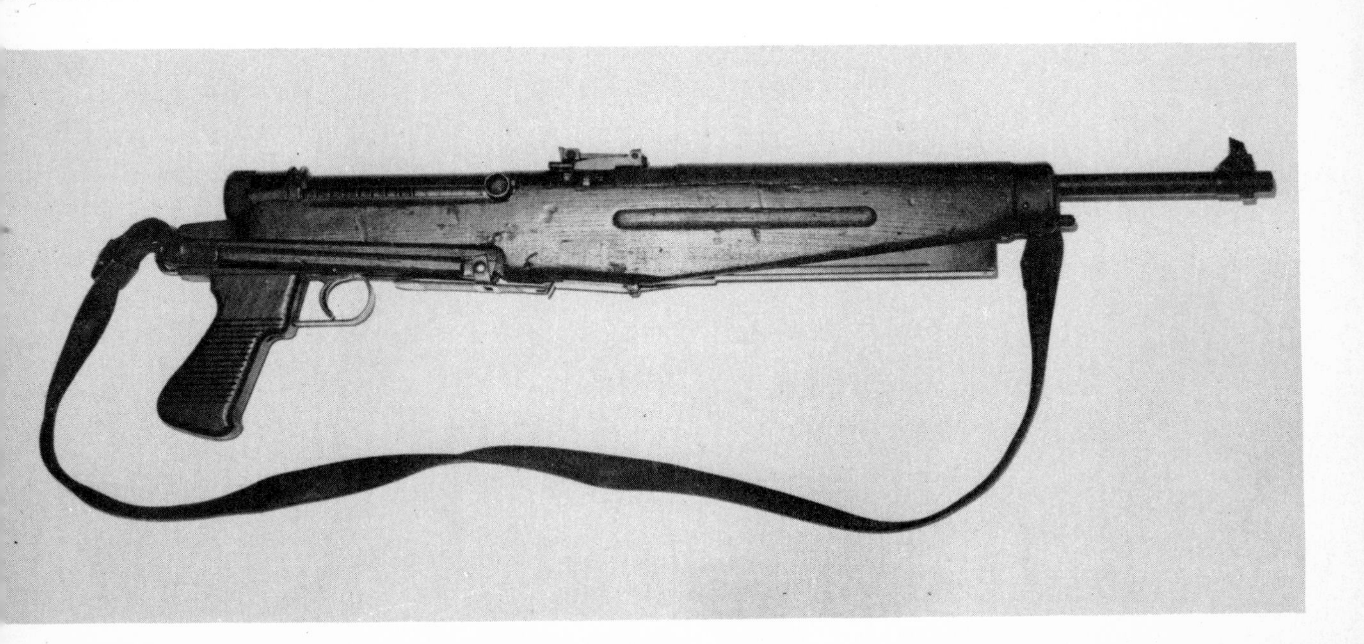

ITALY

Moschetto Automatico OVP

While the mitriaglice leggera Villar Perosa modello 1915 is generally acknowledg
as one of the very first sub-machine guns it was hardly a one-man portable weap
and thus in the 1920s an attempt was made to reduce the number of barrels from tv
to one and the eventual result was the moschetto automatico OVP. This was lit
more than one half of a Villar Perosa fitted to a wooden stock with two triggers – t
front for automatic fire and the rear for single shots. Despite its age the OVP was s
in limited use in 1941 and some numbers were captured during the North Afric
campaigns.

DATA
CALIBRE 9 mm 0.354 in
LENGTH 902 mm 35.5 in
LENGTH OF BARREL 279 mm 11 in
WEIGHT 3.63 kg 8 lb
M.V. 381 m/s 1250 ft/sec
CYCLIC RATE OF FIRE 900 rpm
MAGAZINE CAPACITY 25 rounds

Moschetto Automatico OVP

Moschetto Automatico Beretta modello 1918
Moschetto Automatico Beretta modello 1918/30

In 1918 the Brescia-based firm of Pietro Beretta SpA began a programme c
converting large numbers of Villar Perosa weapons for use by one man. The resul
was the moschetto automatico Beretta 1918. Unlike the OVP the modificatio
incorporated a new set of wooden furniture, an entirely new trigger mechanism, an
a folding bayonet. The mechanism of the Villar Perosa was also modified to incorpo
rate a form of retarded blow-back to slow the rate of fire. The modello 1918 wa
produced in two forms, one with two triggers for automatic and single-shot fire an
one with a single trigger for semi-automatic only.

While the modello 1918 used a top-mounted magazine, the modello 1918/30 wa
revised to take the conventionally-mounted vertical magazine under the body and a
the same time the calibre was changed from the old 9 mm Glisenti cartridge to th
9 mm Parabellum. Both types were still in use in 1941 and saw extensive service.

DATA (modello 1918)
CALIBRE 9 mm 0.354 in
LENGTH 851 mm 33.5 in
LENGTH OF BARREL 317.5 mm 12.5 in
WEIGHT 3.27 kg 7.2 lb
M.V. 389 m/s 1275 ft/sec
CYCLIC RATE OF FIRE 900 rpm
MAGAZINE CAPACITY 25 rounds

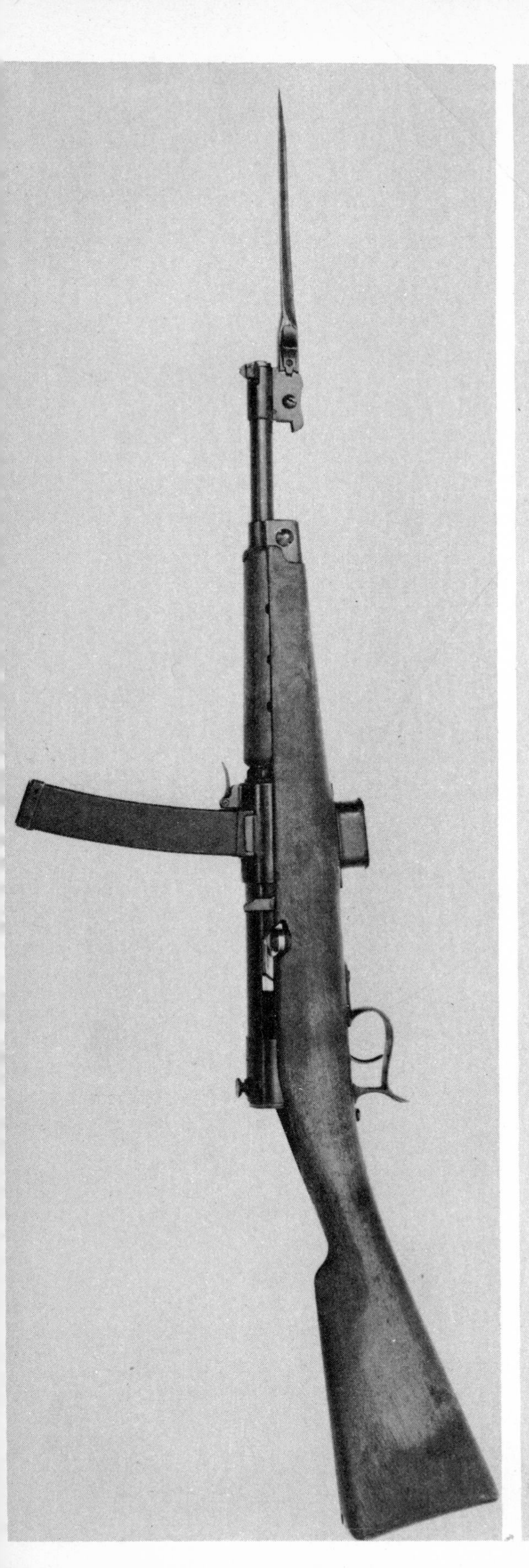

Left: Moschetto Automatico Beretta modello 1918

Right: Moschetto Automatico Beretta modello 1918/30

Moschetto automatico modello 38A

Designed during early 1938 the Beretta modello 38A was one of the most famous and widespread of all the Beretta products. Designed by Tullio Marengoni, it was first issued in 1938 and soon became an immediate success with all who used it, not only for its performance but also for its reliability, due mainly to the excellent standard of workmanship lavished on the design. The first versions used a special cartridge, the 9 mm cartucchia pallottola modello 38A, but later versions were chambered for the conventional 9 mm Parabellum cartridge. This change was brought about by the export success of the modello 38A which was sold to Rumania and several South American states, and after 1941 the modello 38A was also used by the Germans as the 9 mm MP739(i). There were four main production variants, all known as the modello 38A. The first could be fitted with a bayonet and had a simple compensator fitted to the muzzle. The next version had a barrel jacket with holes instead of the former slots – most of the early production versions were in this form. In late 1938 the third variant appeared without the bayonet fitting and a new type of compensator with four slots. The last version appeared during late 1940 and made a small gesture towards mass production needs by having a stamped and welded barrel jacket. Although large numbers of the modello 38A were produced for the Italian forces, large numbers were used by the Germans in Italy and North Africa, and later in the war many fell into the hands of Italian partisans. Elsewhere the modello 38A was used by Jugoslav partisans, and in North Africa it was a favourite weapon for use by raiding parties and the like on the Allied side. However, a general shortage of magazines prevented its widespread use by the Allies.

Second variation of modello 38A, note the 20 round magazine and folding bayonet

DATA

CALIBRE 9 mm 0.354 in
LENGTH 947 mm 37.28 in
LENGTH OF BARREL 320 mm 12.6 in
WEIGHT 3.945 kg 8.7 lb
M.V. (9 mm modello 38A) 450 m/s 1476 ft/sec
M.V. (9mm Parabellum) 420 m/s 1378 ft/sec
CYCLIC RATE OF FIRE 500-600 rpm
MAGAZINE CAPACITY 10, 20 or 40 rounds

Third version of modello 38A with 40 round magazine

Italian troops with modello 38A, third version. Note battle jerkin to carry M.G magazines, identical pockets on the back

oschetto automatico odello 38/42

Moschetto automatico modello 38/42

Good as the modello 38A was, it soon proved to be too difficult and expensive to manufacture in the confines of a wartime economy and as a result the general design was simplified to produce the modello 38/42. Steel stampings were introduced, the barrel jacket was removed, and a new form of dust-protected bolt was fitted. Despite all these simplifications the modello 38/42 was still finished to a high standard, but only 9 mm Parabellum ammunition was used to ease supply problems, of which the Italian forces had more than their fair share. The modello 38/42 was supplied to Rumania and numbers were also produced for German units in Italy and North Africa as the 9 mm MP738(i). The modello 38/43 and modello 38/44 were modified production variants that incorporated gradual production changes to ease manufacture and speed production.

DATA
CALIBRE 9 mm 0.354 in
LENGTH 800 mm 31.5 in
LENGTH OF BARREL 200 mm 7.87 in
WEIGHT 3.27 kg 7.2 lb
M.V. 450 m/s 1476 ft/sec
CYCLIC RATE OF FIRE 550 rpm
MAGAZINE CAPACITY 20 or 40 rounds

Pistola mitriaglice FNA-B modello 1943

DATA
CALIBRE 9 mm 0.354 in
LENGTH – STOCK EXTENDED 790 mm 31.1 in
LENGTH – STOCK FOLDED 526 mm 20.7 in
LENGTH OF BARREL 198 mm 7.8 in
WEIGHT 3.2 kg 7.06 lb
M.V. 373 m/s 1225 ft/sec
CYCLIC RATE OF FIRE 400 rpm
MAGAZINE CAPACITY 20 or 40 rounds

Produced at a time (1943) when Italy was in a state of political and economic ch the FNA-B is an example of what can be achieved when well-trained gunmak build weapons that suit themselves and not a centralised procurement agen Designed by the Fabbrica Nazionale d'Armi of Brescia, the FNA-B was made fr solid steel parts with almost every part machined from the solid. The mechanism us a rather involved delayed blowback brought about by a two-piece bolt. For carryi the butt and magazine folded into a small area, and to end off the design a comp sator was machined into the barrel jacket. The FNA-B was produced for Ital Army and German use but only about 7,000 were made. Undoubtedly one of most expensive sub-machine guns ever to see service the FNA-B was for all its des sophistication an anachronism that had to go when its true economic cost appreciated.

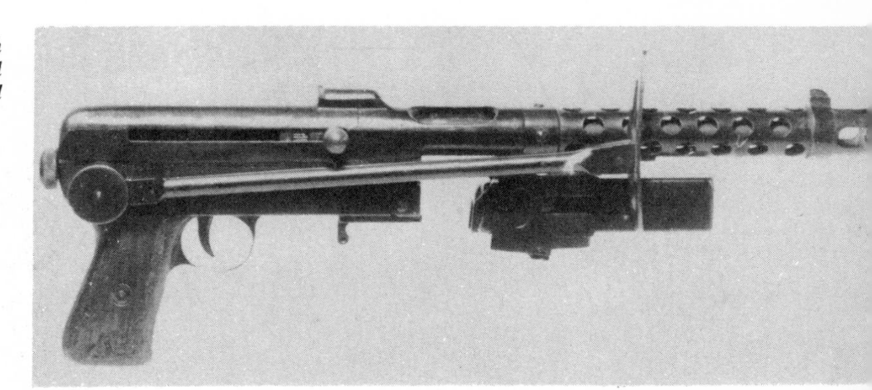

FNA-B with butt and magazine folded

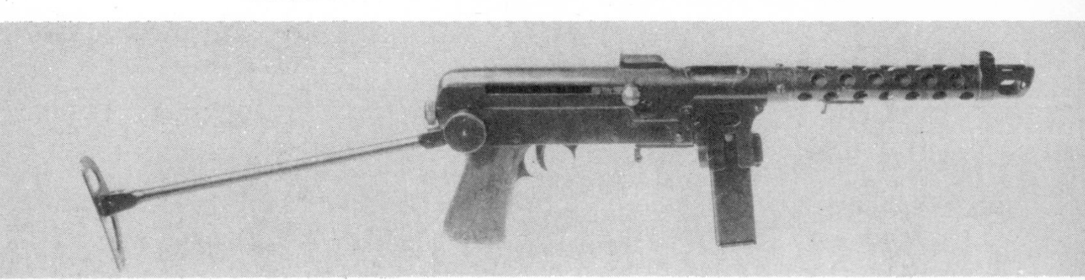

Pistola mitriaglice FNA-B modello 1943

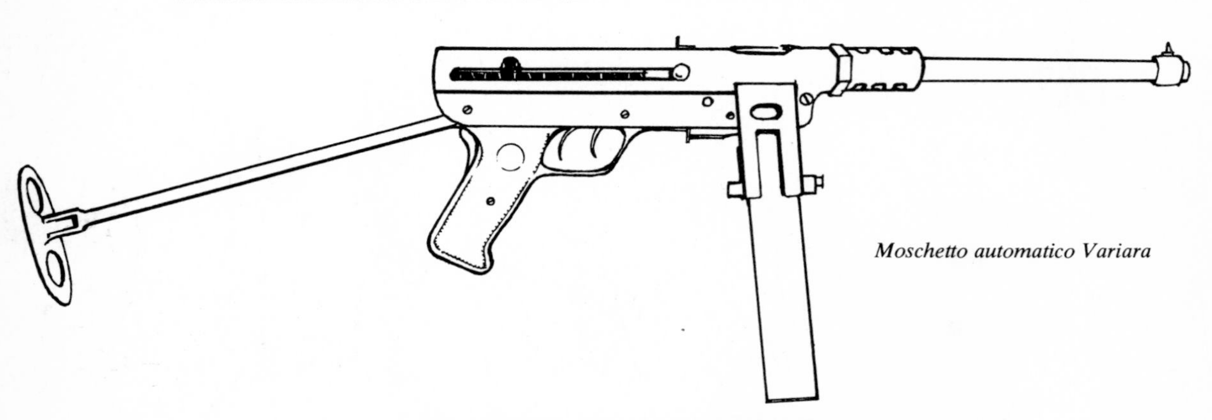

Moschetto automatico Variara

Moschetto automatico Variara

DATA
CALIBRE 9 mm 0.354 in
LENGTH 820 mm 32.3 in
LENGTH OF BARREL 300 mm 11.8 in
WEIGHT 2.815 kg 6.2 lb
M.V. 411 m/s 1350 ft/sec
CYCLIC RATE OF FIRE 550 rpm
MAGAZINE CAPACITY 30 rounds

The Variara sub-machine gun had an unusual provenance in that it was designed a made in a clandestine weapon factory near Biella in Northern Italy. The fi examples were produced in 1943 and until 1945 the small output of the undercov plant went to Italian partisans fighting the occupying German forces. Not surprisin ly, the Variara had few original design features. The Sten was used as a basis but t MP40 grip and safety were incorporated along with the folding butt and magazine the FNA-B. The trigger mechanism came from the Beretta modello 38A.

ITALIAN PORTABLE FLAME-THROWERS

Lanciafiamme, mod 35

At the time of Italy's entry into the war, the Italian Army had in service the Lanciafiamme, mod 35. This had already been used in action against tribesmen in North Africa. The mod 35, which was later used on the Greek-Albanian front, was issued to flame-thrower platoons (Assault (Guastatori) Pioneer Platoons) who operated in conjunction with infantry units, both in defence as well as in attack.

The weapon was served by an operator and an assistant but could only be carried for short distances due to its weight, and because the operator was wearing protective clothing, it was normally transported by truck or mule. The model 35 consisted of two identical cylinders, each containing nitrogen under pressure and fuel oil, and a battery box.

GHT 27 kg 59.4 lb
L 11.8 litres 2.6 gall
NGE 22.8 metres 25 yds
RATION OF FIRE 20 seconds

Lanciafiamme, modello 35

Operators of modello 35 wearing protective clothing

Lanciafiamme, mod 40

The second type of portable flame-thrower used by the Italian Army, especially in North Africa and Russia, was the mod 40. This differed from the mod 35 mainly in its system of ignition.

WEIGHT 27 kg 59.4 lb
FUEL 11.8 litres 2.6 gall
RANGE 16.5 metres 18 yds
DURATION OF FIRE 12 seconds

Lanciafiamme, modello 40 in action in North Africa

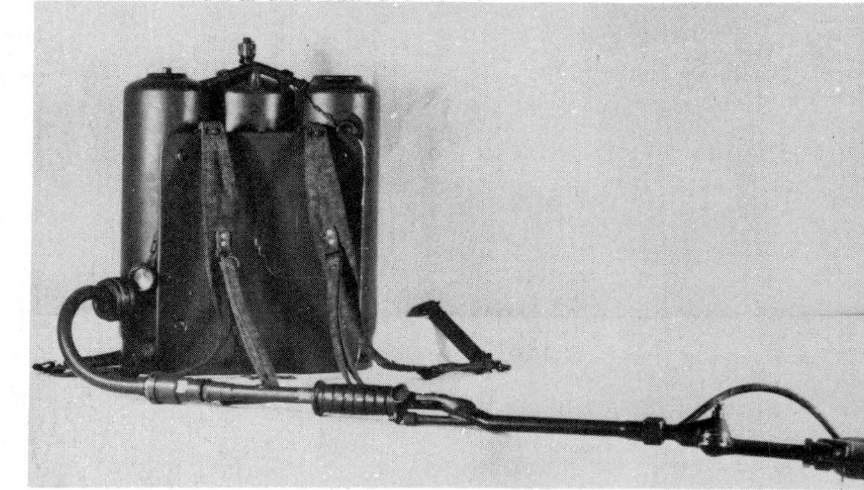

Lanciafiamme, modello 41

modello 41 in action in Tunisia

Lanciafiamme, mod 41

ɪɢʜᴛ 18 kg 40 lb
. 7.95 litres 1.75 gall
ɢᴇ 15.5-20 metres 17-22 yds
ᴀᴛɪᴏɴ ᴏʀ ғɪʀᴇ 5-6 seconds

This model, used chiefly in Tunisia, superseded models 35 and 40 which had become obsolescent due to their excessive weight.

Lanciafiamme, mod 41, consisted of two cylinders of fuel and a cylinder of compressed air, but the quantity of fuel carried was much less than the previous models.

Lanciafiamme, mod 41, d'assalto

ɢʜᴛ 9 kg 19.8 lb
ɢᴇ 20 metres 21.9 yds

This model was developed for assault units; it consisted of a long cylindrical tank containing flammable liquid and gas. At one end was a cap on which the muzzle attachment and the loading port, the turbine-magneto unit was attached to the other end. A pistol grip with a trigger was attached to the body of the tube. The weapon could be fired from the shoulder or from the hip.

Lanciafiamme, modello 41, d'assalto

DATA (Early model)
CALIBRE 8 mm 0.315 in
LENGTH—BUTT EXTENDED 867 mm 34 in
LENGTH—BUTT FOLDED 564 mm 22.2 in
LENGTH OF BARREL 228 mm 9 in
WEIGHT 3.83 kg 8.5 lb
M.V. 335 m/s 1100 ft/sec
CYCLIC RATE OF FIRE 450 rpm
MAGAZINE CAPACITY 30 rounds

DATA (1944 model)
CALIBRE 8 mm 0.315 in
LENGTH 914 mm 36 in
LENGTH OF BARREL 234 mm 9.2 in
WEIGHT 3.83 kg 8.5 lb
M.V. 335 m/s 1100 ft/sec
CYCLIC RATE OF FIRE 800 rpm
MAGAZINE CAPACITY 30 rounds

JAPAN

100 Shiki Kikanshoju

The Japanese Army were somewhat slow in realising the capabilities of the sub-machine gun and up till about 1940 relied on imports of Bergmann sub-machine gun from Europe to provide weapons for trials and special service units. In 1940 the produced the Type 100, produced in two forms. One, with a fixed butt, was made at Kokura Arsenal and a further version with a folding butt for paratroop use was made at Nagoya. The Type 100 fired the Japanese 8 mm pistol round at automatic only. The design was not a great success and remained undeveloped, and poor ammunition was a constant source of trouble. About 10,000 of the fixed butt version and 7,500 of the folding butt variant were produced.

Ease of production was not one of the Type 100's better points and in 1944 an attempt was made to rectify this. Welding and other such 'short cuts' were introduced but this late model Type 100 was little different from earlier models other than that its finish was very poor, and even crude. Rate of fire was increased.

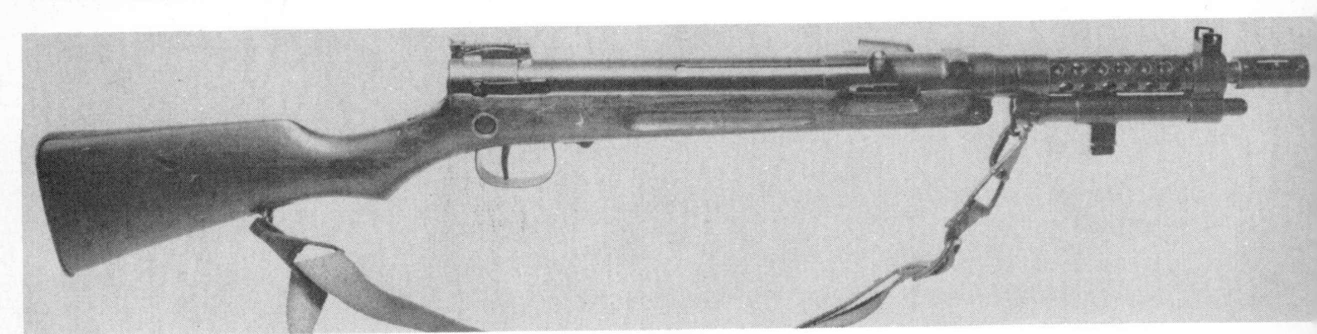

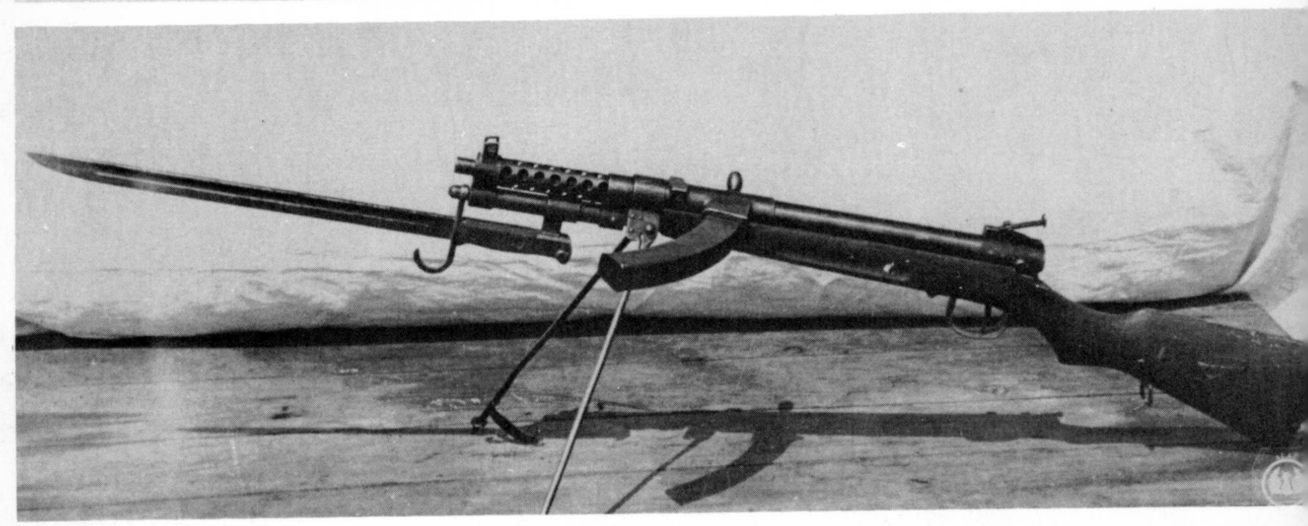

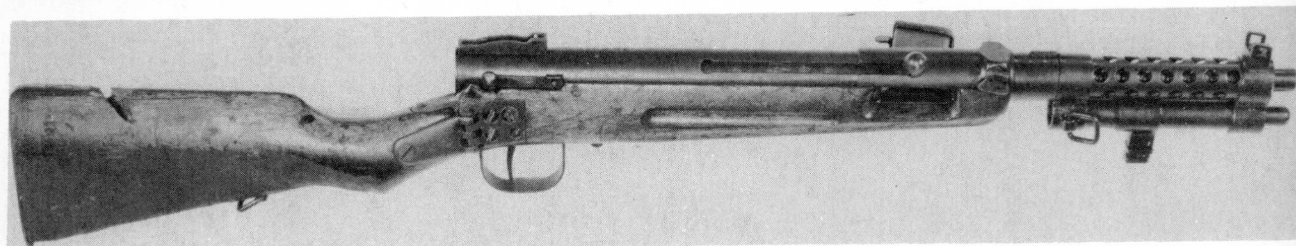

Top: 100 Shiki Kikanshoju (1940)

Centre: Type 100 (1940) with bipod and model 30 bayonet

Above: Paratroop Type 100 (1940)

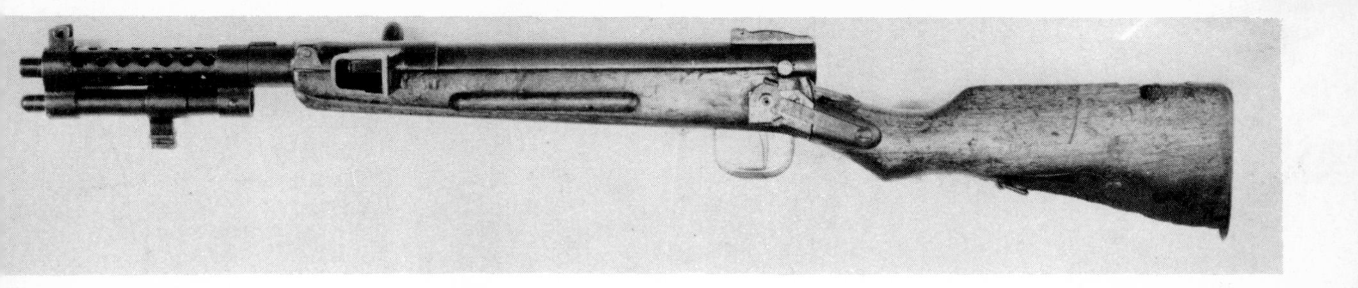

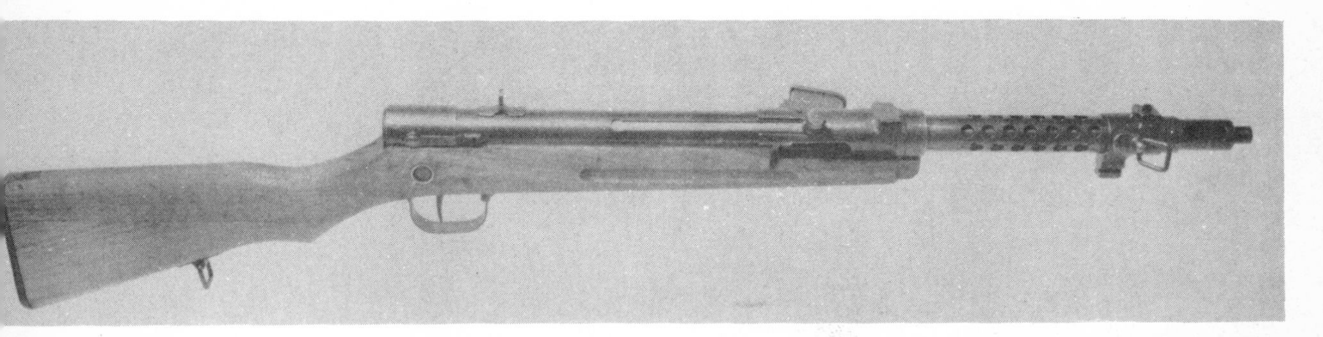

ɔp: Paratroop type 100 (1940)

ɓove: Type 100 (1944)

JAPANESE PORTABLE FLAME-THROWERS Models 93 and 100

Two types of portable flame-thrower were standard in the Japanese Army, the Model 93 and the Model 100. Since there was little difference between the construction of these two types, they could be regarded as identical weapons. Both models consisted of two fuel tanks and a nitrogen pressure tank. A modification in the flame gun of Model 100 was the only difference.

WEIGHT 25 kg 55 lb
FUEL 14.77 litres 3.25 gall
RANGE 22.9-27.4 metres 25-30 yds
DURATION OF FIRE 10-12 seconds

odel, 93

Japanese flame-thrower attack on the Corregidor fortress

ROMANIA

9 mm Orita M.1941

Romania obtained a number of Beretta sub-machine guns from Italy prior to 1941 so it was not particularly surprising that when the Romanian designer Leopold Jaska put forward a sub-machine gun design, it had certain visual similarities with the Italian weapon. The Romanian design was put into production at Cugir Arsenal as the Orita M.1941 and the entire output was directed to the Romanian Army who adopted it as their standard service arm and used it extensively on the Russian Front. Operation was simple blowback and the rearsight was a very prominent recognition feature. Production ceased during 1944, by which time some production examples were being manufactured with folding metal butts in place of the usual well-made wooden butts.

DATA
CALIBRE 9 mm 0.354 in
LENGTH 894 mm 35.2 in
LENGTH OF BARREL 287 mm 11.3 in
WEIGHT 3.46 kg 7.625 lb
M.V. 390 m/s 1280 ft/sec
CYCLIC RATE OF FIRE 400-600 rpm
MAGAZINE CAPACITY 25 or 32 rounds

9 mm Orita M.1941

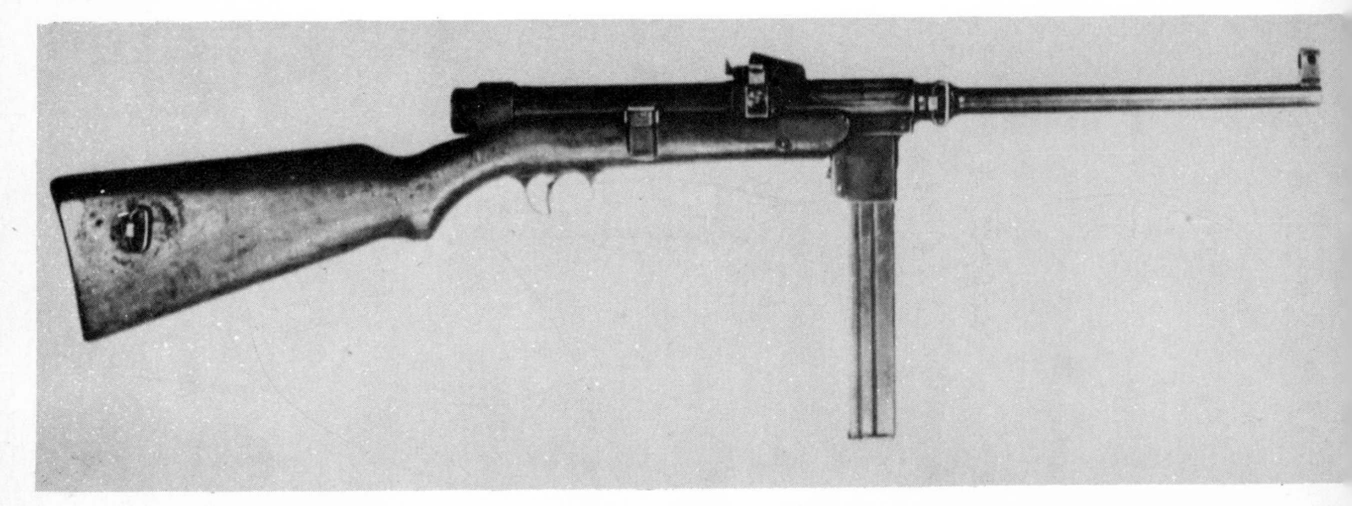

Machine Carbine, 9 mm Lanchester Mark 1 and 1*

During 1941 it was decided to adopt a sub-machine gun for use by the Royal Navy and Royal Air Force. Sten production was almost exclusively assigned to the Army, so an alternative design was sought, and a product of the Sterling Engineering Company was decided upon. This product was the Lanchester Machine Carbine which took its name from its 'designer' G.H. Lanchester, but the design was an almost exact copy of the German MP28/11. The Lanchester was a very well made and solid weapon, so well made that the magazine housing was solid brass. One change that was made to suit British needs was that the stock was the same as that used on the Rifle No. 1 Mark III*, and a bayonet could be fitted to the muzzle. Early examples, the Mark 1 versions, had a selector mechanism but this was removed on the Mark 1* and most Mark 1 versions were eventually converted to Mark 1* standard. Almost all the output of 100,000 went to the Royal Navy and Commonwealth navies – the Royal Air Force decided not to adopt the Lanchester and used the Sten. Production ceased before the war ended.

ATA
ALIBRE 9 mm 0.354 in
ENGTH 851 mm 33.5 in
ENGTH OF BARREL 200 mm 7.9 in
EIGHT 4.343 kg 9.65 lb
.V. 366 m/s 1200 ft/sec
YCLIC RATE OF FIRE 600 rpm
AGAZINE CAPACITY 50 rounds

anchester Mk.I

Machine Carbine, 9 mm Sten Mark 1 and 1*

After Dunkirk the British Army was in desperate need of weapons to re-equip, and the need for some form of sub-machine gun was high on the list of priorities. Two designers, Shepperd and Turpin, at the Royal Small Arms Factory, Enfield, submitted a design that was accepted for production under the name Sten, from the initials of the two designers and the factory. The Sten was based on experience gained from the German MP40 in that it was intended for cheap and easy mass production in very large numbers. Almost every component was designed for manufacture with a minimum of machining or pressing and extensive use was made of sub-contractors. The first production example, the Mark 1, entered service in the summer of 1941 and met with a less than enthusiastic response mainly due to the Sten's rough and crude appearance, but in action it was found to be efficient enough, even though the magazine feed system did give trouble – this feed problem was never completely eradicated from the whole Sten range of Marks. The Mark 1 had a flash hider and a wooden fore-stock and grip but these were removed on the Mark 1* which went into production in late 1941, and over 100,000 examples of the Mark 1 and 1* were made.

DATA
CALIBRE 9 mm 0.354 in
LENGTH – Mark 1 895 mm 35.25 in
LENGTH – Mark 1* 794 mm 31.25 in
LENGTH OF BARREL 198 mm 7.8 in
WEIGHT – Mark 1 3.561 kg 7.84 lb
WEIGHT – Mark 1* 3.235 kg 7.125 lb
M.V. 366 m/s 1200 ft/sec
CYCLIC RATE OF FIRE 540 rpm
MAGAZINE CAPACITY 32 rounds

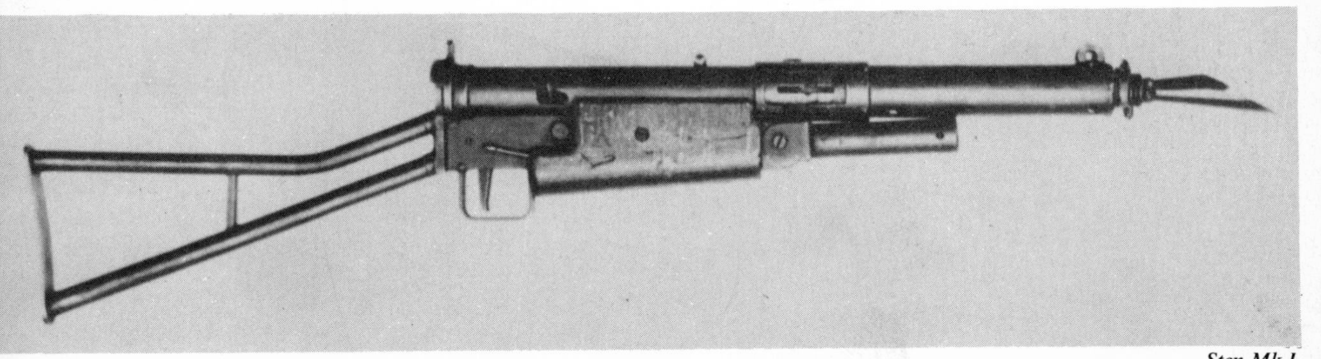

Sten Mk.I

Machine Carbine, 9 mm Sten Mark 2

DATA
CALIBRE 9 mm 0.354 in
LENGTH 762 mm 30 in
LENGTH OF BARREL 197 mm 7.75 in
WEIGHT 3 kg 6.625 lb
M.V. 366 m/s 1200 ft/sec
CYCLIC RATE OF FIRE 540 rpm
MAGAZINE CAPACITY 32 rounds

While the Sten Mark 1 was a simple weapon, the Mark 2 was even simpler. On th Mark 2 every part was produced as the simplest and cheapest part that could do th job required. For instance the barrel was held in place by a screw-on jacket and wa usually a drawn steel tube with only two rifling grooves (later the number of groove was increased to six). The barrels, as all the other parts, were made by sub contractors on very simple machines in a large number of workshops and factorie and the Mark 2 was also produced in Canada and New Zealand (small numbers onl in New Zealand). Operation was by simple blow-back as in the Mark 1 and th trigger mechanism was a very simple device. For all its simplification the Sten Mark was a remarkably efficient weapon. It could be quickly and easily stripped fo cleaning or concealment and the magazine housing could be rotated to keep dirt fron the ejection port. More Sten Mark 2s were made than any other Mark and the fina total ran to over 2,000,000. They were issued to all arms of the services and ver large numbers were dropped into occupied Europe to arm the resistance and partisa forces that formed during the German occupation. With these forces the Sten Mark showed itself to be an excellent weapon. It could be easily concealed, easily operate and was easy to maintain. Some resistance forces went to the extent of making thei own Stens, as in Denmark, and the Sten was indeed widely copied. Copies were mad in China and the Germans even went to the level of producing the MP3008, a almost exact imitation. The Sten certainly impressed the German forces. Larg numbers were used by occupation forces as the MP 749(e), mainly culled fron captured resistance stocks, but the most bizarre German use of the Sten came wit the Gerät Potsdam. This was produced by Mauser in 1944 and it was an exact copy o the Sten Mark 2, copied exactly down to the British markings. These were appar ently intended for use by some form of German guerilla arm but although abou 25,000 were made (at very great expense and diversion of facilities) they were littl used.

Canadian soldier holds a Sten Mk.2 produced in Canada

Machine Carbine, 9 mm Sten Mark 2 (Silencer)

ATA
ALIBRE 9 mm 0.354 in
NGTH 908 mm 35.75 in
NGTH OF BARREL 91.7 mm 3.61 in
EIGHT 3.42 kg 7.547 lb
.V. 305 m/s 1000 ft/sec
CLIC RATE OF FIRE 450 rpm
AGAZINE CAPACITY 32 rounds

The Mark 2(S) version of the Sten was a variant produced to equip special forces that required some form of weapon that was almost completely silent. The Mark 2(S) was produced for this purpose and had a special breech block and spring. The barrel was short and surrounded by sound insulation that meant almost complete silence when the weapon was fired. It was intended for single shot use only with the fully automatic facility for emergency use alone. The Mark 2(S) was used extensively by Commando units and some were dropped into occupied Europe – some of these ended up in German hands as the MP 751(e).

ten Mk.II(S)

Machine Carbine, 9 mm Sten Mark 3

DATA
ALIBRE 9 mm 0.354 in
ENGTH 762 mm 30 in
ENGTH OF BARREL 197 mm 7.75 in
VEIGHT 3.18 kg 7 lb
M.V. 366 m/s 1200 ft/sec
YCLIC RATE OF FIRE 540 rpm
MAGAZINE CAPACITY 32 rounds

The Sten Mark 3 was really a version of the Mark 1 revised to simplify manufacture even further. Internally the mechanism was the same but on the Mark 3 the barrel was a permanent fixture in a tubular housing and the magazine housing could not rotate. Nearly every part was a simple pressing or tubular assembly and spot welding and rivetting was extensively used. The Mark 3 was produced in large numbers in the United Kingdom and Canada and was issued widely. It was a crude unlovely weapon but it was efficient and proved its worth throughout the world.

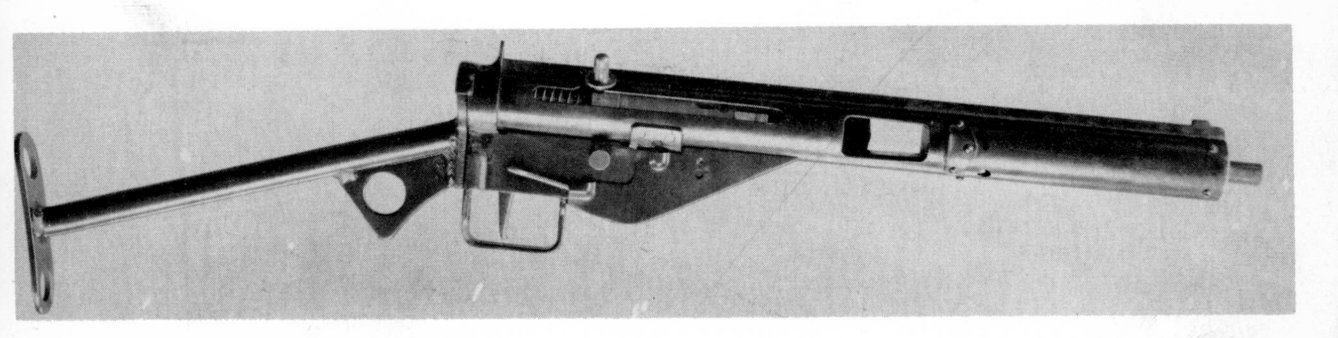

Sten Mk.III

Machine Carbine, 9 mm Sten Mark 5

The Sten Mark 4 was an experimental weapon intended for paratroop use but it did not go into production, so after the Mark 3 the next service Mark was the Mark 5. It was first made in 1944 at a time when production pressures were somewhat eased and thus some 'extras' could be fitted to the basic Sten design. The most obvious addition was the wooden stock, pistol grip and foregrip. A bayonet could be fitted to the muzzle and the foresight from the No. 4 rifle was fitted. Overall machining standards were considerably improved and the finish was much better than that of the earlier Marks. The result, the Sten Mark 5, was one of the best sub-machine guns used during World War 2 and a far cry from the earlier Marks 1 to 3. Originally issued to airborne troops the use of the Mark 5 spread to all the other arms of the services and it remained in use for some years. In service the foregrip was often removed.

DATA
CALIBRE 9 mm 0.354 in
LENGTH 762 mm 30 in
LENGTH OF BARREL 198 mm 7.8 in
WEIGHT 3.9 kg 8.6 lb
M.V. 366 m/s 1200 ft/sec
CYCLIC RATE OF FIRE 540 rpm
MAGAZINE CAPACITY 32 rounds

Sten Mk.V

Sten Mk.V with No.4 Mk.II spike bayonet

Machine Carbine, 9 mm Sten Mark 6

The Sten Mark 6 was a silenced version of the Mark 5 along the same lines as the earlier Mark 2(S). It was similar in operation to the earlier Mark but relatively few were made.

DATA
CALIBRE 9 mm 0.354 in
LENGTH 857 mm 33.75 in
LENGTH OF BARREL 95 mm 3.75 in
WEIGHT 4.32 kg 9.5 lb
M.V. 305 m/s 1000 ft/sec
CYCLIC RATE OF FIRE 450 rpm
MAGAZINE CAPACITY 32 rounds

Sten Mk.VI

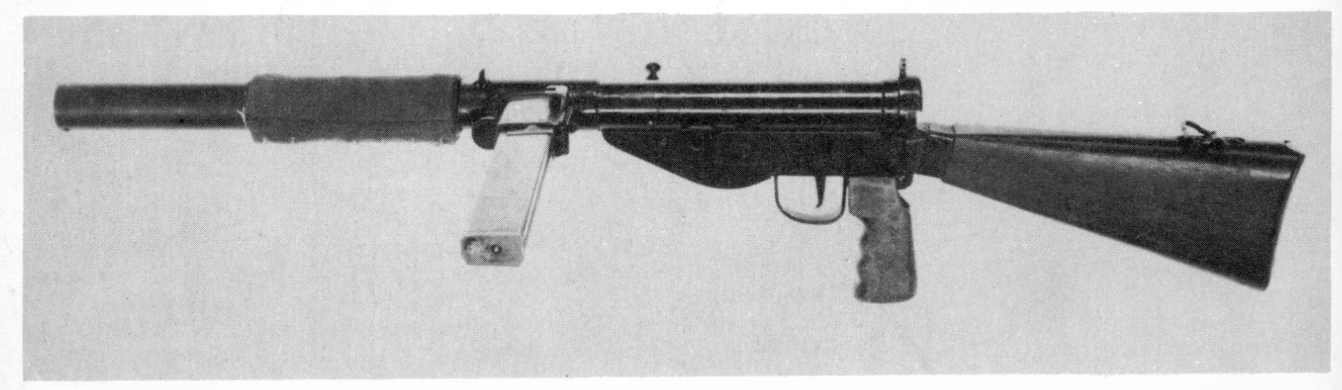

BRITISH PORTABLE FLAME-THROWERS
The Marsden

(Flame-Thrower, Portable, No. 1, Mark I)

In 1939 no flame-throwing equipment was available as a service weapon and, by 1940, the Army soon realised that such a weapon would be required by the infantry in close fighting and for clearing strong points. Work was therefore put in hand to develop such a weapon and this resulted in the 'Marsden'. This consisted of four fuel cylinders and a pressure cylinder connected to flame-gun similar in shape to that of a rifle. The 'Marsden' was sent for troop trials in the United Kingdom and the Middle East and proved to be heavy and unreliable. With the development of the 'Lifebuoy' it became obsolete.

DATA
WEIGHT 38.1 kg 84 lb
FUEL 18.2 litres 4 gall
RANGE 18-23 metres 20-25 yds
DURATION OF FIRE 12 seconds

Flame-Thrower, Portable, No. 1, Mk.I

The Marsden under test

The 'Lifebuoy'

(Flame-Thrower, Portable, No. 2, Marks I and II)

WEIGHT 29 kg 64 lb
FUEL 18.2 litres 4 gall
RANGE 27.4-36.5 metres 30-40 yds
DURATION OF FIRE 10 seconds

Development of this equipment was begun in 1941; it consisted of a fuel container of lifebuoy shape with a spherical pressure container in the centre connected to a lightweight flame gun. This weapon was similar in design to that of the German 1940 pattern. In May 1942 a pilot model was ordered for trials and this was followed shortly after by an order, but early 1943 defects became apparent during trials and so the Mk. I was relegated to training units.

In the autumn of 1943 a modified design, the Mk. II, was introduced but this did not reach full production until early in 1944. Production of the Mk. II ceased in July 1944.

Flame-Thrower, Portable, No.2 Mk.I

The 'Harvey'

(Flame-Thrower, Transportable, No. 1, Mark I)

FUEL 127.3 litres 28 gall
RANGE 46-55 metres 50-60 yds
DURATION OF FIRE 12 seconds

Developed as a transportable static flame-thrower for the defence of Great Britain after Dunkirk, the 'Harvey' was a crude and simple equipment. It consisted of a fuel tank and a compressed cylinder mounted on a two-wheeled carriage, a handle was attached to the fuel container to enable this equipment to be pushed like a wheelbarrow.

In action the fuel left the tank via a 30-ft length of flexible hose which was held by the crew and directed at the target. Many of these were issued to the Home Guard during the 'invasion scare'. Some of them were later sent to Middle East where they were adapted for smoke production. They were never used in a flame role.

Flame-Thrower, Transportable, No.1, Mk.I

USA

Thompson Model 1928

DATA
CALIBRE 11.43 mm 0.45 in
LENGTH (with compensator) 857 mm 33.75 in
LENGTH OF BARREL 267 mm 10.52 in
WEIGHT 4.88 kg 10.75 lb
M.V. 280 m/s 920 ft/sec
CYCLIC RATE OF FIRE 600-725 rpm
MAGAZINE CAPACITY 20, 30 or 50 rounds

The weapon that was eventually to emerge as the infamous 'Tommy Gun' was originally intended for the trench fighting of 1918, but delays in development of the early prototypes delayed the first production models until 1921. In that year the Thompson Model 1921 was offered for commercial sale but sales were few. The design was owned by the Auto-Ordnance Corporation, but the original work was done by J. T. Thompson who had several small-arms designs under his name before he started work on a hand-held automatic weapon. The Model 1921 was produced in some numbers. It was a retarded blowback weapon that was chambered for the standard .45 pistol cartridge. It could take a number of differing magazines the largest of which was a 100-round drum magazine but this was not a great success. The more usual magazines were a 50-round drum and a 20-round vertical box magazine. But as already mentioned sales were few and a later model the Model 1928 was merely the Model 1921 with a few modifications such as a muzzle-fitted compensator (the Cutts Compensator which had a small measure of success in preventing the muzzle from rising when the gun was fired). This Model 1928 was produced in small numbers for the US Navy only, but in 1939 large numbers were ordered by the French Army, and in late 1939 by the British Army. Thereafter the Model 1928 began to come off the production lines as the British order was raised from an initial 450 to quite simply as many as could be made and delivered – large numbers from this order ended up on the bed of the Atlantic as the U-boat campaign got underway. After 1940 the French weapons ended up in German hands as the MP760(f), but other weapons came to the German armoury by way of the overrun Baltic states (some went to Russia). Prior to 1941 a batch was delivered to Jugoslavia just in time for the German invasion and a further addition to the German total as the MP760(j). The British weapons were issued not only as Home Guard weapons but also as front-line issue and as the war went on many were handed out to second-line units and many Commonwealth forces. Back in the USA the Model 1928 was issued to cavalry units as the M1928A1, and some were issued to the US Coastguard, but the numbers involved were small. There were several variations on the Model 1928. Some were issued without the compensator, some did not have the wooden foregrip, and there were several internal changes. In service the 50-round drum proved noisy and was replaced by the box magazine, but the main fault of the Model 1928 was its cost in money and manufacturing facilities as it was a complex weapon. But in 1939 and 1940 it was all that was available and it was produced in thousands.

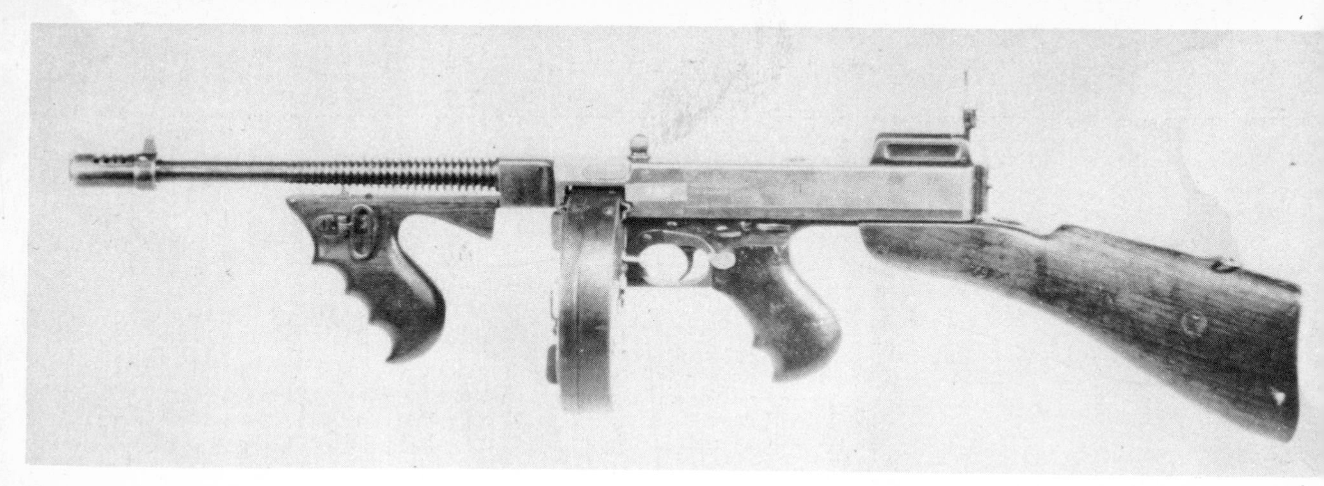

Thompson Model 1928A1 with vertical foregrip and 50 round drum magazine

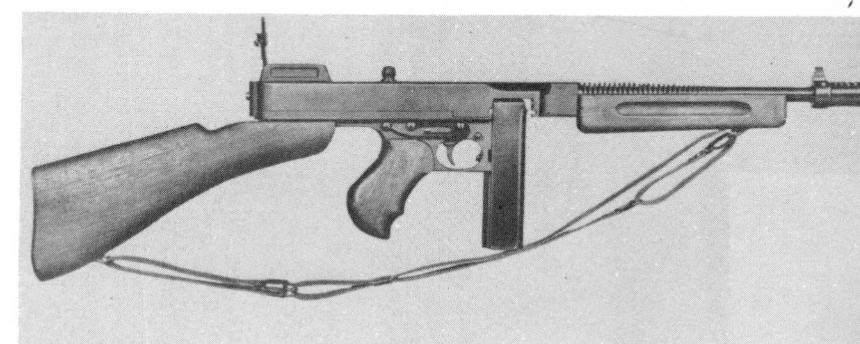

Thompson Model 1928A1 with horizontal foregrip and 20 round box magazine

U.S Marine in New Britain, armed with the Thompson Sub-machine gun

Sub-machine gun, Caliber .45, M1 and M1A1

As the Thompson Model 1928 soon proved itself to be an expensive weapon to produce attempts were soon made to reduce its complexity. The need for this reduction in cost was coupled with a need for rapid production as even by late 1940 the US Army was still without any form of sub-machine gun except for a few M1928A1's. The Model 1928 was thus modified into a simpler blowback weapon with the removal of such extras as the removable butt stock, the barrel fins and compensator. As the 50-round drum had proved to be noisy and cumbersome in European service the modified design could only take the 20- or 30-round box magazines. In this form the Thompson became the Sub-machine gun, Caliber .45, M1 and it remained in production until 1945 by which time well over 1,000,000 had been made. A further simplification was made to produce the M1A1 which had a fixed firing pin in place of the earlier separate firing pin and hammer. In service the M1 and M1A1 were very popular weapons and were often preferred to the later M3 and such weapons as the Sten. Large numbers were issued to Allied forces, especially in the Far East where the Chinese went so far as to make their own copies (they also made copies of the Model 1928).

TA
BRE 11.43 mm 0.45 in
GTH 813 mm 32 in
GTH OF BARREL 267 mm 10.52
GHT 4.74 kg 10.45 lb
280 m/s 920 ft/sec
LIC RATE OF FIRE 700 rpm
AZINE CAPACITY 20 or 30 rounds

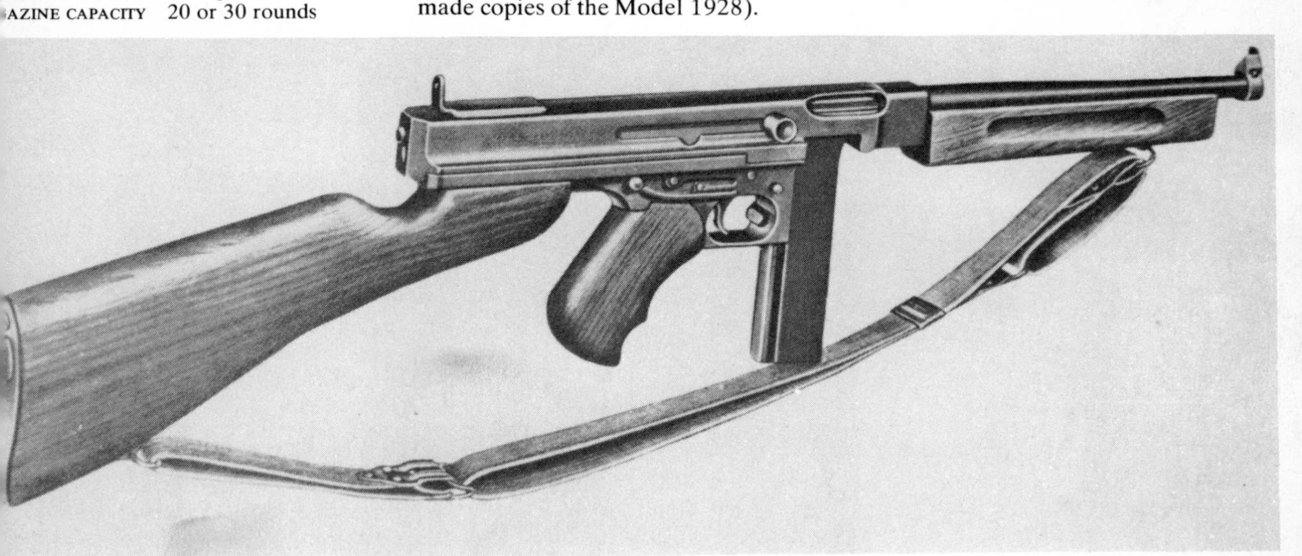

e MIAI

U.S Marine with MIAI, in action on Okinawa

Sub-machine gun, Caliber .45, M2

DATA
CALIBRE 11.43 mm 0.45 in
LENGTH 815 mm 32.1 in
LENGTH OF BARREL 307 mm 12.1 in
WEIGHT 4.2 kg 9.25 in
LENGTH OF BARREL 293 m/s 960 ft/sec
CYCLIC RATE OF FIRE 500 rpm
MAGAZINE CAPACITY 20 or 30 rounds

During 1941, George Hyde completed the development of a weapon that was result of a string of experimental sub-machine guns. It was produced under auspices of the Inland Division of General Motors and was thus known as 'Hyde-Inland'. This weapon was submitted for official trials and selected for proc tion as the M2 sub-machine gun. Production was contracted to the Marlin Firea Corporation but relatively few were produced as the M2 was soon found tc difficult to produce in numbers and the type was overtaken by the later M3 declared obsolete in June 1943. Despite this the few that were manufactured v issued to airborne and similar special forces. The M2 had few design points of no it was an accurate weapon in its class and it was easy to use, but in 1942 spee production was an overriding factor so the M2 pased from the scene.

Caliber 45, M2

Sub-machine gun, Caliber .45, M3

During 1942 the US Army held trials on a number of different sub-machine g none of which completely satisfied their requirements. One of the sub-machine g tested was the British Sten which was favourably commented upon but it was selected for US production. Instead the Aberdeen Proving Grounds staff took idea of a simple mass-produced weapon and produced the T15. This became, af trials, the T20, and in this form was submitted to rigorous testing until selected service as the M3. The M3 closely followed the Sten concept but had several chang One change was in the feed which was a vertical 30-round box based on that used the German MP40. In service the M3 met with the same acceptance difficulties as the Sten in British Army service, but when its odd appearance had become m familiar it soon proved itself to be reliable and efficient. Production of the M3 v handed out to a number of contractors and sub-contractors, many with little expe ence of small-arm production but as the M3 incorporated a large number of sim stampings and the like this mattered little. By 1945 606,694 had been produc Most of these went to the US forces but some were dropped into occupied Eurc and the Far East and for this purpose a special 9 mm conversion kit (comprising barrel, bolt and magazine housing to take a Sten magazine) was produced but f appear to have been used. Another extra was a silencer, and another an optio flash hider. Fire was automatic only with no facility for single shot, but a lit experience enabled single shots to be 'squeezed-off'.

DATA
CALIBRE 11.43 mm 0.45 in
LENGTH – STOCK EXTENDED 757 mm 29.8 in
LENGTH – STOCK RETRACTED 579 mm 22.8 in
LENGTH OF BARREL 203 mm 8 in
WEIGHT 3.7 kg 8.15 lb
M.V. (approx) 280 m/s 920 ft/sec
CYCLIC RATE OF FIRE 350-450 rpm
MAGAZINE CAPACITY 30 rounds

ber 45, M3

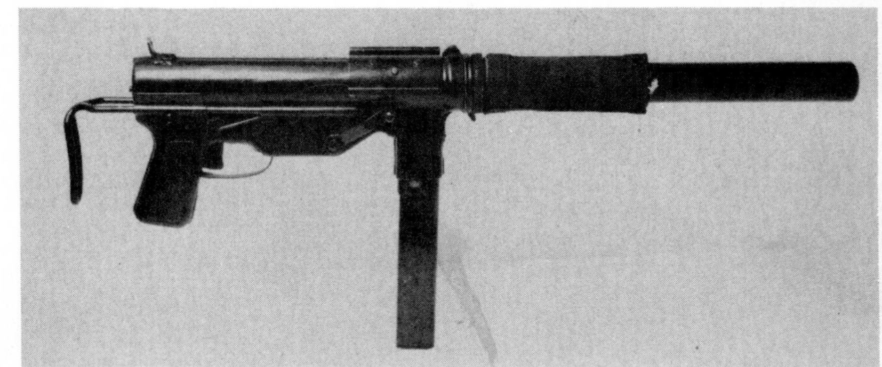

M3 with Silencer

enth U.S Army patrol in Northern Alsace
ed with the M3 Sub-machine gun, the
n in front carries a MI Carbine

Sub-machine gun .45, M3A1

Simple as the M3 was it soon became apparent that simplification could be carrie stage further and at the same time cure one of the weaknesses of the M3. On the ea production M3's the bolt retracting handle often broke in use. To cure this the M3 did away with the handle altogether and the M3A1 was cocked by putting a fin into a hole in the bolt and drawing it back. Other changes were a magazine saf cach to prevent the magazine falling out too easily and an enlarged ejector p More minor changes included an oil can in the pistol grip. Production of the M3 started in December 1944 and during 1945 15,469 were made. In service it did li to eleviate the general dislike of the M3 sub-machine gun as for all its success it usually denigrated in favour of the Thompson or M1 carbine. Nevertheless the and M3A1 were widely copied by many nations after 1945.

DATA
As M3

Reising Model 50 and 55

DATA (Model 50)
CALIBRE 11.43 mm 0.45 in
LENGTH 908 mm 35.75 in
LENGTH OF BARREL 279 mm 11 in
WEIGHT 3.06 kg 6.75 lb
M.V. 280 m/s 920 ft/sec
CYCLIC RATE OF FIRE 550 rpm
MAGAZINE CAPACITY 12 or 20 rounds

The Reising sub-machine gun was one of the number submitted to the US force 1940 and 1941, but unlike so many submitted designs the Reising actually s production. Designed by Eugene G. Reising, production was carried out by Harri ton & Richardson in late 1941 and most of the output went to the US Mari although others were sold to the UK and Canada, and a few were sent to Russia. T Reising Model 50 was unusual in several respects one of which was that it fired fro closed bolt. Cocking was effected by drawing back a catch under the forestock, a the mechanism was unduly complex even though it was a basic blowback system. T complexity not only made the Model 50 expensive to manufacture but in action mechanism jammed at the ingress of even small amounts of dirt or grit. Despite these faults the Reising sub-machine gun remained in small-scale production u 1945 and about 100,000 were made. The Model 55 was similar in most respects the Model 50 but had a folding wire butt and no compensator. It was issued to the Marines but was not any more successful in service than the Model 50.

Reising Model 55

Reising Model 50

U.S Parachute Troopers armed with the Reising Model 55

United Defense Corporation Model 1942

TA

IBRE	9 mm 0.354 in
GTH	820 mm 32.3 in
GTH OF BARREL	279 mm 11 in
GHT	4.14 kg 9.12 lb
.	400 m/s 1312 ft/sec
LIC RATE OF FIRE	700 rpm
GAZINE CAPACITY	2 × 20 rounds

Although the UD M.'42 was not accepted for service with any service arm it nevertheless saw action in many odd corners and in many odd situations. Developed from a string of sub-machine guns designed by Carl G. Swebilius, the UD M.'42 was the production version of the Model 41. It was offered to the Dutch and British governments, and the Dutch placed an order for issue to the forces in the Dutch East Indies. Some were delivered before the Japanese overran the area and thereafter the M.'42 was manufactured by the Marlin Firearms Company for the Office of Strategic Services (OSS). From there the M.'42 was sent off on many clandestine missions in the Far East, Europe and the Mediterranean theatre. Small numbers were used by British undercover forces where it was generally known as the 'Marlin'. The M.'42 was a very well made weapon that featured a reversible pair of magazines. Total production was about 15,000.

U.D.M 42

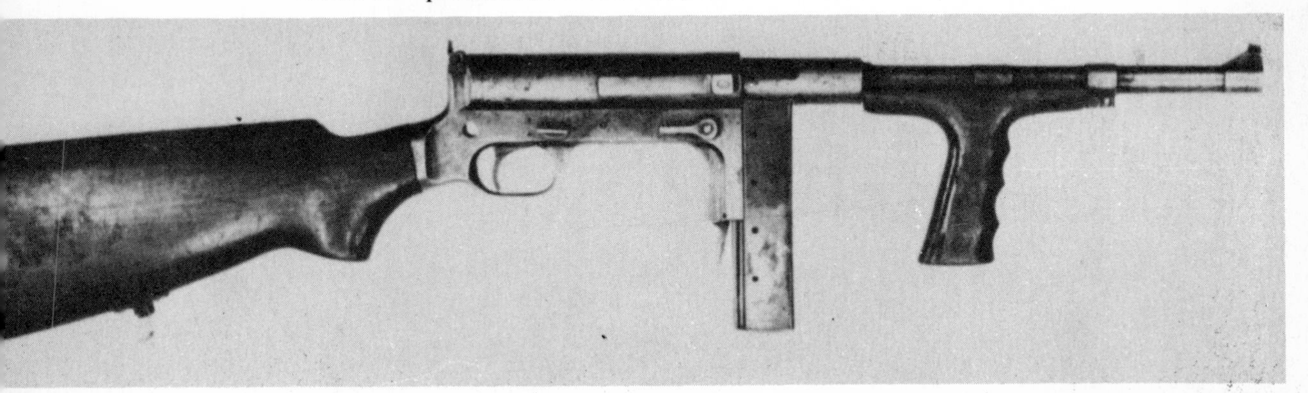

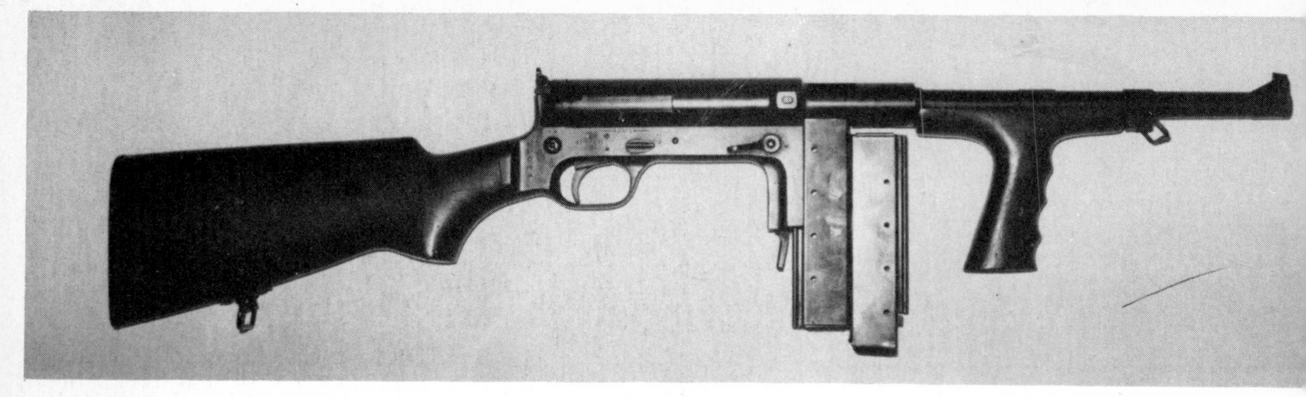

U.D.M 42 with reversible magazines

Rifle, Caliber .30, M1

The Rifle M1 has the distinction of being the first self-loading rifle to be taken in service as a standard weapon by any service arm. It was accepted as a standard rifle the US Army in 1932 and thereafter it was gradually issued to all the various arms the American forces. By 1941 the full changeover from the Rifle M1903 was still n complete but by 1945 over 5,5000,000 had been made. The M1 was almost unive sally known as the 'Garand' after its designer John C. Garand. It was a very w made weapon that was rather expensive to manufacture but in service it prov reliable and sturdy, and as proof of the soundness of the design it has remain virtually unchanged since the very first production model. There have been ma experimental versions, but only two were produced in any quantity. These were t M1C and the M1D, both sniper rifles. The M1 was a gas-operated rifle which tapp off gas from near the muzzle to operate an actuating piston. Ammunition was f from an eight-round clip which was ejected when the last round was fired. This c was perhaps the M1's only fault as it meant single rounds could not be loaded 'top-up' the magazine and the sound of the clip ejecting advertised the fact that t rifle was empty – a sound often listened for by an enemy at close quarters. But t fault could not detract from the overall success of the Garand, a fact testified by t use of captured examples by the Germans (as the Selbstladegewehr 251(a)) and the Japanese imitation of the design for their 7.7 mm Rifle Type 5 – only prototyp of the latter were made before the war ended.

DATA
CALIBRE 7.62 mm 0.30 in
LENGTH 1107 mm 43.6 in
LENGTH OF BARREL 609 mm 24 in
WEIGHT 4.313 kg 9.5 lb
M.V. 855 m/s 2805 ft/sec
MAGAZINE CAPACITY 8 rounds

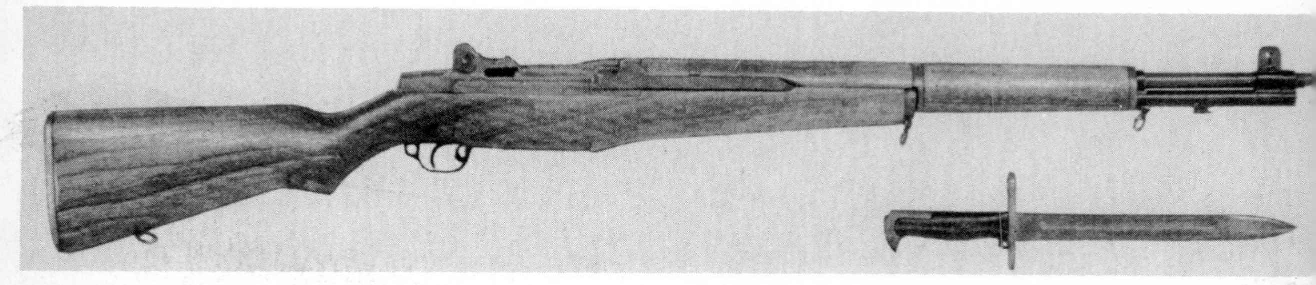

Rifle, Caliber .30, M1

Carbine, Caliber 30, M1

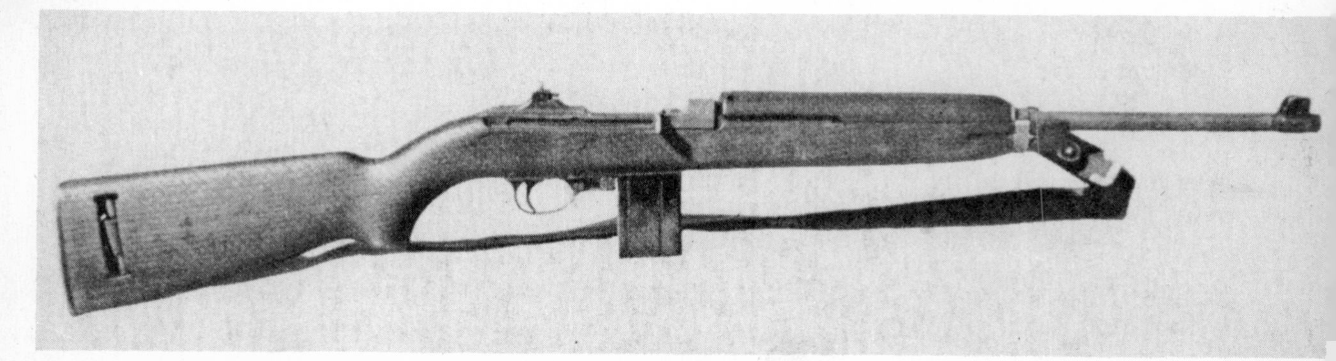

U.S soldiers with M1 rifles attack Japanese dugout

Carbine, Caliber .30, M1 and M1A1

The usual arm for second-line troops and for such soldiers as machine-gunners in the US Army was usually some form of pistol before 1941. In 1940 a request was made for some form of self-loading carbine, and in late 1940 a series of trials began with a number of designs submitted. The eventual winner of these trials was a Winchester carbine, adopted as the Carbine M1. The M1 had a unique gas-operated mechanism, and it soon proved to be a very popular weapon, so popular that the eventual production total ran to millions and more Carbines were made during World War 2 than any other American weapon (total of all Carbine versions was over 6,332,000). In time the Carbine M1 was carried not only by the second-line and support arm troops for which it was intended but also by front line combat troops. It had one main drawback and that was the special cartridge that it fired. This proved to be under-powered but was nevertheless produced in huge quantities. The one major variant of the M1 was the M1A1 which differed only in having a folding stock for use by paratroops and airborne units. Captured weapons were impressed by the Germans as the Selbstladekarabiner 455(a) and issued to units operating behind the American lines during the Ardennes offensive of late 1944.

ATA (M1)
LIBRE 7.63 mm 0.30 in
NGTH 904 mm 35.6 in
NGTH OF BARREL 457 mm 18 in
EIGHT 2.36 kg 5.2 lb
V. 600 m/s 1970 ft/sec
GAZINE CAPACITY 15 or 30 rounds

ATA (M1A1)
s M1 except:
NGTH – STOCK EXTENDED 901 mm 35.5 in
NGTH – STOCK FOLDED 645 mm 25.4 in
EIGHT 2.8 kg 6.19 lb

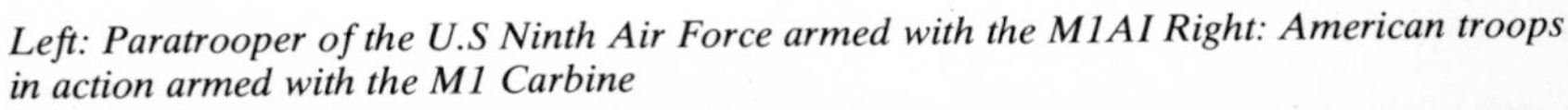

Left: Paratrooper of the U.S Ninth Air Force armed with the M1A1 Right: American troops in action armed with the M1 Carbine

Carbine, Caliber .30, M2

Carbine, Caliber .30, M2 and M3

The original specification for the Carbine M1 called for the ability to fire automatically but this was dropped in order to get the design into production quickly. Winchester had however built the fully-automatic capacity into the M1 design so that when the call for an automatic ability came from the field, this call could be quickly and easily met. The result was the Carbine M2 which differed from the M1 only in having a selector mechanism on the left side near the trigger, and a curved box magazine holding 30 rounds could be used – this magazine could also be used on the M1. The Carbine M3 was a version of the M2 which could be fitted with an infra-red night-sight but very few (just over 2,000) were made and they were not very widely used – a flash hider was also fitted.

DATA (M2)
CALIBRE 7.62 mm 0.30 in
LENGTH 904 mm 35.6 in
LENGTH OF BARREL 457 mm 18 in
WEIGHT 2.36 kg 5.2 lb
M.V. 600 m/s 1970 ft/sec
CYCLIC RATE OF FIRE 750-775 rpm
MAGAZINE CAPACITY 15 or 30 rounds

Johnson Semi-automatic Caliber .30 M1941 Rifle

Soon after the M1 Garand rifle started its production run a new contender as standard service rifle for the US forces appeared on the scene in the form of the Johnson Model MR-2, Type R. This excellent design was the work of Melvin M. Johnson, USMC, and it had several unusual features. One was a quick-change barrel, another a rotary magazine, and the mechanism incorporated a rotary locking mechanism. The Johnson rifle seemed to have many advantages over the Garand rifle and at one time a great deal of publicity was given to the case for adoption of the Johnson design. But the US Army decided to keep the M1 in production and the few service models that were produced for the American forces went to the US Marines. Others were sold to Chile (a total of 1000 chambered for the 7 mm Mauser round) and a large batch was sold to the Dutch East Indies. In service the Johnson proved to be too delicate a weapon for the rigours of service life, but this did not prevent the design from being developed into the Johnson Light Machine Gun.

DATA
CALIBRE 7.62 mm 0.30 in
LENGTH 1165 mm 45.87 in
LENGTH OF BARREL 559 mm 22 in
WEIGHT 4.3 kg 9.5 lb
M.V. (approx) 844 m/s 2770 ft/sec
MAGAZINE CAPACITY 10 rounds

Opposite page: Johnson Semiautomatic Caliber .30 M1941 Rifle

Indonesian troops of the Netherlands forces armed with Johnson Rifles and Thompson sub-machine guns

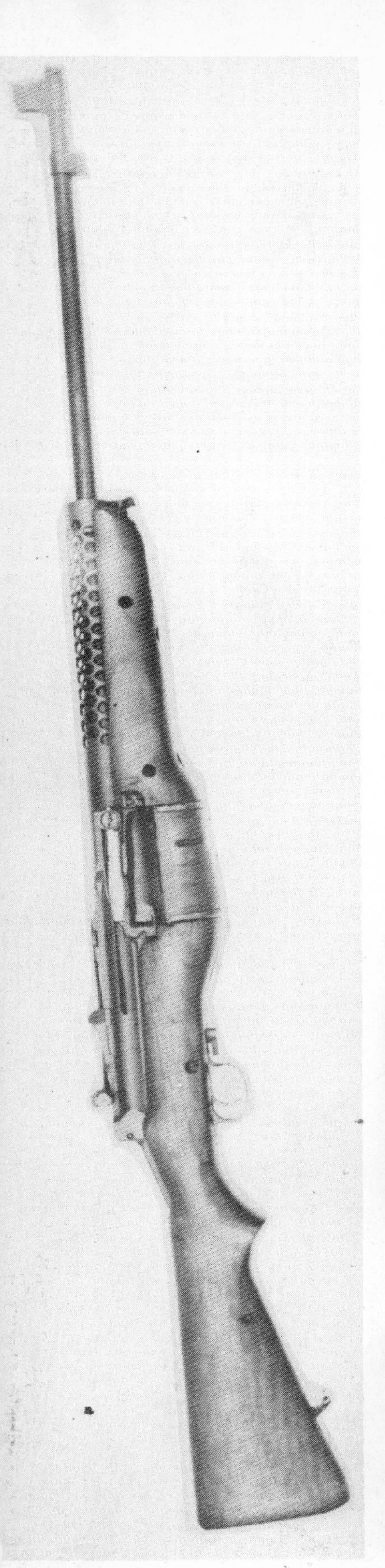

AMERICAN PORTABLE FLAME-THROWERS

The US Army during WW2 used three basic types of portable flame-throwers: the M1, M1A1 and the M2-2; though an earlier prototype model, the E1R1, had been used in Papua and North Africa. All these models were identical in appearance, consisting of two fuel tanks and a pressure tank.

Due to the jungle terrain that provided cover for the flame-thrower operators, allowing them to make their way forward to an effective range, and to the no-surrender resistance of the Japanese soldier who often dug-in and fought to the death, the portable flame-thrower was used more often in the Pacific campaigns by the US forces than in the European theatre.

Portable Flame-Thrower, M1

This was developed from the earlier E1R1. The M1 was put into production in March 1942 and was employed for the first time on Guadalcanal, 15 June 1943.

WEIGHT 31.8 kg 70 lb
FUEL 18.2 litres 4 gall
RANGE 22.9-27.4 metres 25-30 yds
DURATION OF FIRE 8-10 seconds

Portable Flame-Thrower, M1A1

In the summer of 1942 the M1 was modified to allow the use of the newly developed thickened fuel, the resulting model M1A1 was used extensively during 1942 and 1943 in the Pacific war. Range increased to 45-50 yds.

Portable Flame-Thrower, M2-2

When certain basic deficiencies appeared in the M1A1 a new model was produced, the M2-2. This version was adopted in March 1944 and was first employed in the Guam operations in July 1944. Production of this model was greater than of the other two models combined.

WEIGHT 30.9-32.7 kg 62-72 lb
FUEL 18.2 litres 4 gall
RANGE 22.9-36.5 metres 25-40 yds
DURATION OF FIRE 8-9 seconds

Portable Flame-thrower, M1 being used against Japanese buildings in the Marshalls

Above: Portable Flame-thrower, EIRI undergoing tests

Right: Demonstration of the MIAI

Below: Portable Flame-Thrower, M2-2

PPD, 1934/38 with box magazine

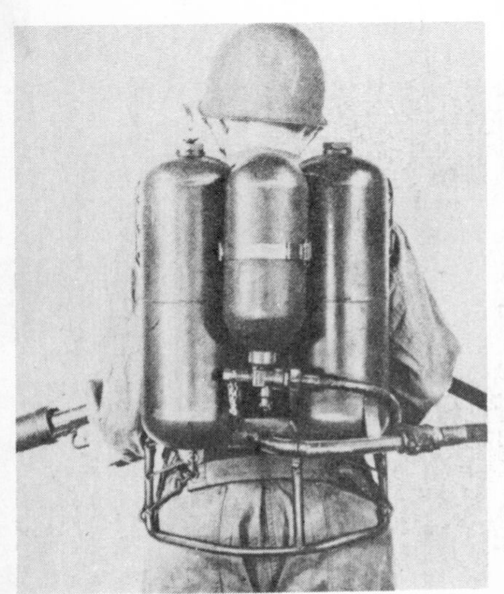

US Marine uses M2-2 flame-thrower against Japanese strong-point on Okinawa

USSR

Pistolet-Pulemet Degtyareva o1934/38g

First introduced into service in 1934, this sub-machine gun was the work of V.A. Degtyarev. It was often referred to as the PPD, and its design used features of the Suomi m/1931 and the German MP28/11. The first model used a 73-round magazine but on the second production model a 71-round magazine, copied from the Finnish Suomi magazine, was fitted. A further production version used a simpler barrel jacket with fewer and larger slots cut into it. Production of the PPD was carried out at Tula and Sestrorjetsk arsenals and production appears to have ceased in 1940. The PPD was a conventional blowback weapon and its construction had little of note other than that the barrel was chromed to increase its service life – this became a standard Russian practise on later designs. After 1941 the PPD was captured in sufficient numbers to enter German use as the MP716(r). As well as using captured Russian ammunition, the Germans also made use of 7.63 mm Mauser ammunition as the German round was dimensionally almost identical to the Russian round – this applied to all the Russian sub-machine guns used by the Germans.

ATA
LIBRE 7.62 mm 0.30 in
NGTH 777 mm 30.6 in
NGTH OF BARREL 273 mm 10.75 in
EIGHT 3.74 kg 8.25 lb
.V. 488 m/s 1600 ft/sec
CLIC RATE OF FIRE 800 rpm
AGAZINE CAPACITY 25 (box) or 71 rounds (also 73)

Pistolet-Pulemet egtyareva o1934/38g

Pistolet-Pulemet Degtyareva o1940g

First used in action during the 1940 campaign in Finland, the obrazets 1940 was an improvement of the earlier PPD. It was designed with a view to easier production but it was still made of good well-made parts and for this reason it was not kept in production after the German invasion of 1941. Many parts of the 1940 were interchangeable with the earlier o1934/38 but a new 71-round drum magazine was used and the bolt was different. The method of fitting this magazine was also different as it was placed into a recess on the front of the receiver rather than being pushed up into the gun as in the earlier model. This weapon was often known as the PPD1940 but those used by the Germans were known to them as the MP715(r).

ATA
ALIBRE 7.62 mm 0.30 in
ENGTH 787 mm 31 in
ENGTH OF BARREL 267 mm 10.5 in
EIGHT 3.63 kg 8 lb
.V. 488 m/s 1600 ft/sec
YCLIC RATE OF FIRE 800 rpm
AGAZINE CAPACITY 71 rounds

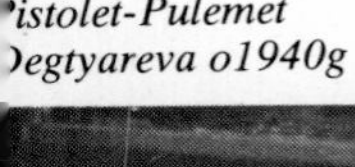

istolet-Pulemet Degtyareva o1940g

Red Army Guardsmen with PPD, 1940, in action on Leningrad front

Soviet soldier in action with PPS 1941, note box magazine

Pistolet-Pulemet Shpagina o1941g

DATA

CALIBRE	7.62 mm 0.30 in
LENGTH	840 mm 33.07 in
LENGTH OF BARREL	269 mm 10.6 in
WEIGHT	3.5 kg 7.7 lb
M.V.	488 m/s 1600 ft/sec
CYCLIC RATE OF FIRE	900-1000 rpm
MAGAZINE CAPACITY	35 or 71 rounds

During the German invasion of 1941 the Russians lost not only vast amounts of equipment but also much of their industrial capacity. Thus the Russians were in a similar position to the British after Dunkirk and they too needed a sub-machine gun that could be turned out quickly, cheaply and easily. The Russian answer was a design by G.S. Shpagin that was to be known as the PPSh or PPSh1941. It was adopted during 1941 but the first production models did not reach the troops until 1942. After that it was turned out in tens of thousands so that by 1945 over 5,000,000 had been made. The PPSh was a simple weapon that could be produced with a minimum of machine tools, and the finish of many was crude. But in use it was very efficient and its strong construction made it reliable under all conditions. The one concession to quality was that the barrels remained chromed even when at one stage they were made by simply cutting old rifle barrels in half. In service the PPSh was often handed out to all arms of the services and often whole units were equipped with it up to battalion level, and the PPSh was often the weapon employed by the famous 'Tank Descent' formations. The PPSh made a great impression on the Germans who used as many as they could capture. They even went to the extent of converting many to 9 mm Parabellum by fitting new barrels and magazine housings to take the MP40 magazine. The German designation for these 9 mm conversions is unknown but unconverted weapons were known as the MP717(r).

Pistolet-Pulemet Shpagina o1941g

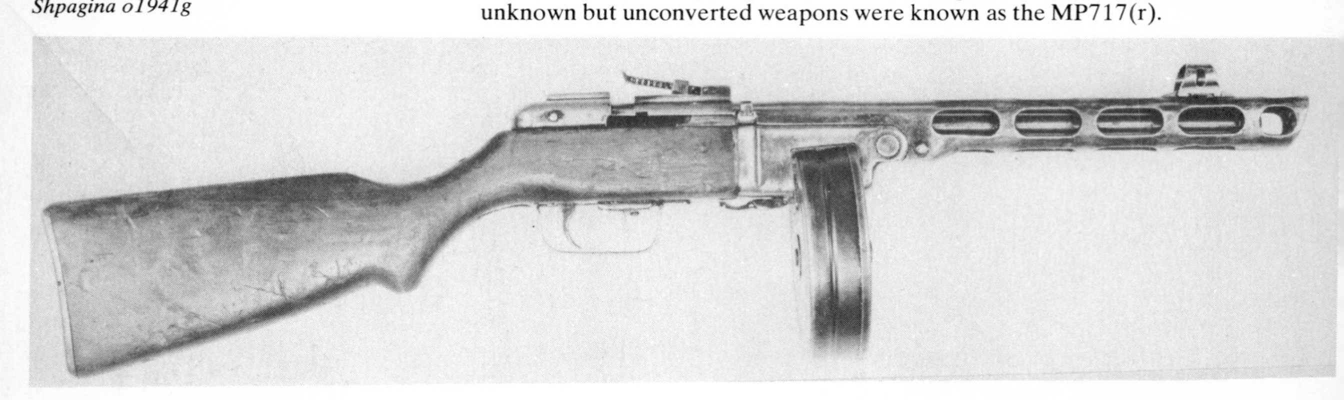

PPS, 1942 with metal butt folded

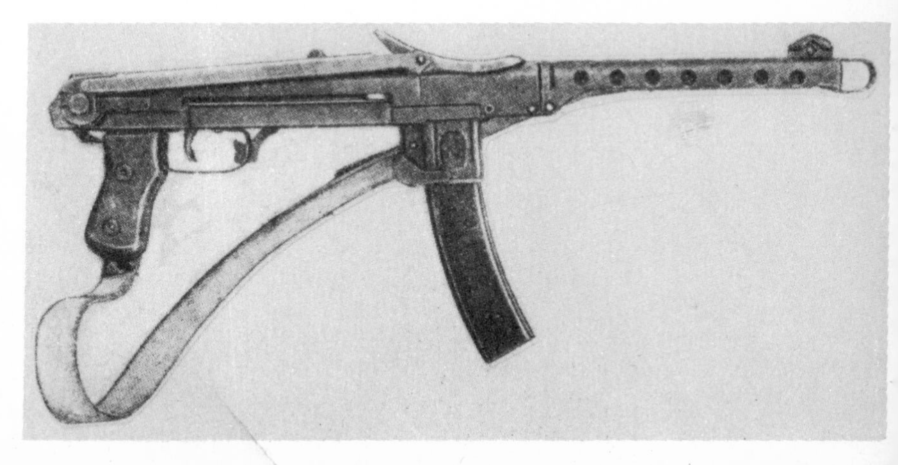

Pistolet-Pulemet Sudareva o1942g

DATA
CALIBRE 7.62 mm 0.30 in
LENGTH – STOCK EXTENDED 907 mm 35.7 in
LENGTH – STOCK FOLDED 641 mm 25.25 in
LENGTH OF BARREL 273 mm 10.75 in
WEIGHT 3.33 kg 7.34 lb
M.V. 488 m/s 1600 ft/sec
CYCLIC RATE OF FIRE 700 rpm
MAGAZINE CAPACITY 35 rounds

Few weapons can have been produced under such desperate conditions as the PPS42 for it was designed and made in the city of Leningrad during 1942. Leningrad was cut off by the Germans soon after they invaded Russia in 1941 and from then on few supplies could reach the units defending the city. Weapons soon began to run low but a military engineer, A.I. Sudarev, produced a sub-machine gun the main features of which were dictated by the machine tools available. This weapon, soon to be known as the PPS42, was made almost entirely of heavy steel stampings with all fixings being made with spot welds, pins or simple rivets. Wood or plastic was used on the pistol grips only, and a folding metal butt was used in place of the usual Russian wooden butt. The first prototypes were tested in the front lines of the city defences where it proved to be a very useful weapon and the design proved sound in action. After Leningrad was relieved the PPS42 was kept in production and improved to become the PPS43.

Pistolet-Pulemet Sudayeva o1942g

Pistolet-Pulemet Sudareva o1943g

DATA
CALIBRE 7.63 mm 0.30 in
LENGTH – STOCK EXTENDED 820 mm 32.28 in
LENGTH – STOCK FOLDED 623 mm 24.5 in
LENGTH OF BARREL 254 mm 10 in
WEIGHT 3.04 kg 6.7 lb
M.V. 488 m/s 1600 ft/sec
CYCLIC RATE OF FIRE 700 rpm
MAGAZINE CAPACITY 35 rounds

The soundness of the design of the PPS42 and the ease with which it could be produced meant that it was kept in production after the Siege of Leningrad had been lifted. Some changes were introduced however, and the end result was the PPS43. This differed from the PPS42 in several respects, most of which were changes to make the design even simpler to produce. The safety mechanism was improved and the metal stock shortened. Other changes were to the magazine housing and the pistol grips were made of hard rubber. Some internal changes were made and the method of production dictated some other visual alterations, especially on the simple compensator fitted over the muzzle. The PPS43 was kept in production until after 1945 by which time about 1,000,000 had been made. Some were used by the Germans as the MP709(r). In Finland a copy in 9 mm Parabellum was made for the Finnish Army as the m/1944.

Pistolet-Pulemet Sudayeva o1943g

PPS, 1943 with metal butt folded

Russian soldiers armed with captured Submachine guns. Left: the Finnish Suomi, Right: the German Erma

Avtomaticheskaia Vintovka Simonova o1936g

DATA
CALIBRE 7.62 mm 0.30 in
LENGTH 1234 mm 48.6 in
LENGTH OF BARREL 614 mm 24.16 in
WEIGHT (less magazine) 4.05 kg 8.93 lb
M.V. 840 m/s 2756 ft/sec
MAGAZINE CAPACITY 15 rounds

The first self-loading rifle issued to the Red Army was the AVS (or AVS36). Desig work started during the early 1930s but despite extended development the AVS wa not a success. The designer was S.G. Simonov, and the AVS was a gas-operate weapon. Its precise tactical role does not appear to have been very well specified as selector mechanism was fitted to enable it to be used in the light machine gun role, role the AVS was not suited to carry out as it suffered from excessive muzzle blast t the extent that a rather poor compensator/muzzle brake had to be fitted. Anothe problem was that the bolt handle flew back and forth in an open slot which not onl provided a hazard to the firer but allowed the ingress of dirt to jam the rathe complex mechanism. As a result of these defects the AVS was withdrawn from us after about 1938 but in 1941 there were still some numbers in service, mainly wit second-line units. Captured examples were used in small numbers by the Germans a the S1Gew 257(r). Small numbers of the AVS were issued to Red Army sniper unit – these were fitted with telescopic sights.

Avtomaticheskaia Vintovka Simonova o1936g

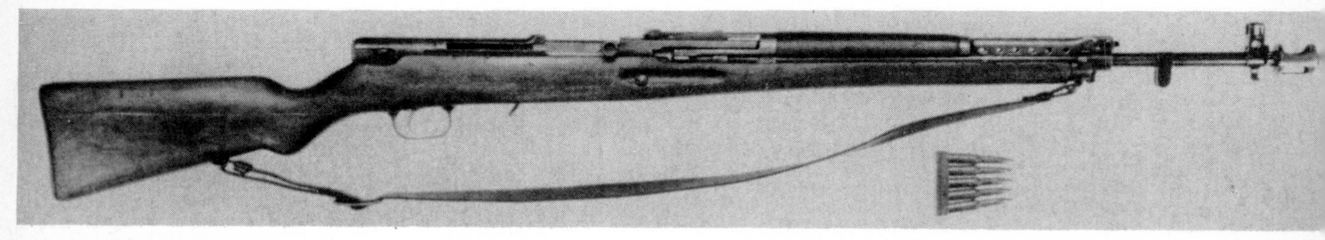

Samozariadnyia Vintovka Tokareva o1938g

DATA
CALIBRE 7.62 mm 0.30 in
LENGTH 1222 mm 48.1 in
LENGTH OF BARREL 635 mm 25 in
WEIGHT 3.95 kg 8.7 lb
M.V. 830 m/s 2723 ft/sec
MAGAZINE CAPACITY 10 rounds

The AVS was replaced in service as a self-loading rifle by the SVT38 which was a design by F.V. Tokarev. The mechanism was another gas-operated system with the gas tapped off over the barrel, and a two or six-baffled muzzle brake was fitted. Like the AVS the SVT38 had several failings. Despite the muzzle brake the weapon had a heavy recoil, but its main failing was that so much attention had been concentrated on reducing weight that the overall construction was not up to the knocks and handling of normal service life. Also the mechanism was very prone to breakdown and maintenance was not easy. As a result production ceased in 1940, but not before some selected weapons had been fitted with telescopic sights for sniper work. Some numbers of the SVT38 fell into German hands as the S1Gew 258(r) and these were used against their former owners.

Samozariadnyia Vintovka Tokareva o1938g

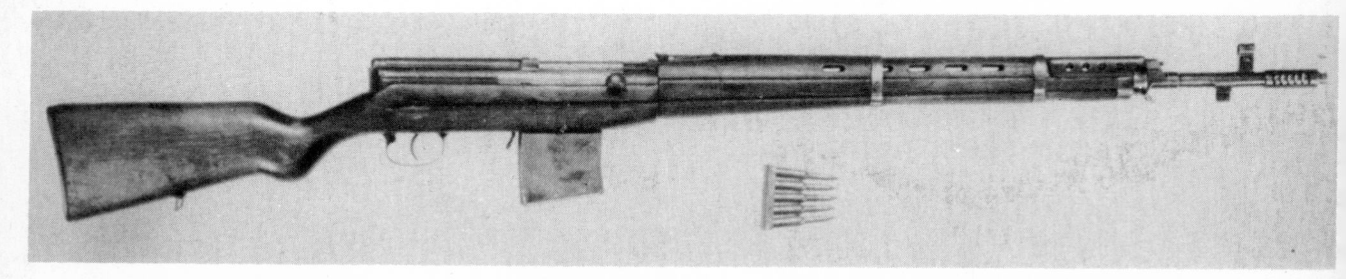

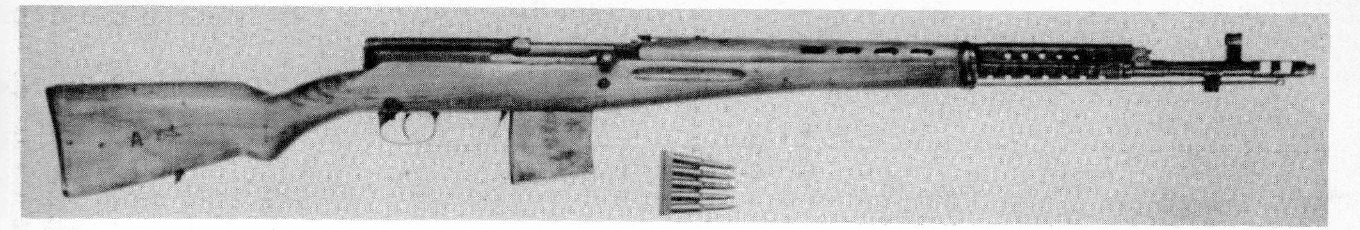

Samozariadnyia Vintovka Tokareva o1940g late production model

Samozariadnyia Vintovka Tokareva o1940g Avtomaticheskaia Vintovka Tokareva o1940g

DATA
CALIBRE 7.62 mm 0.30 in
LENGTH 1222 mm 48.1 in
LENGTH OF BARREL 625 mm 24.6 in
WEIGHT (SVT40) 3.89 kg 8.56 lb
WEIGHT (AVT40) 3.8 kg 8.375 lb
M.V. 830 m/s 2723 ft/sec
MAGAZINE CAPACITY 10 Rounds

Experience with the SVT38 showed that the basic mechanism was good but the construction was too flimsy, so as many things as could be put right were incorporated into the SVT 40. This was basically the same as the SVT38 but the strengthened mechanism and components meant that the SVT40 was a much better weapon. It was still a rather unpopular weapon as it retained the heavy recoil but it did add to the firepower of the infantry, and most were issed to NCOs. Selected weapons were fitted with telescopic sights, and a further variation came with a carbine version which was either converted from existing weapons or manufactured on the production lines – very few of these carbines appear to have been made. Yet another variant was the AVT40 which differed only in having a selector mechanism to fire full automatic. Again, very few of these appear to have been made. The SVT made quite an impact on the invading Germans as they adopted the basic Tokarev mechanism for their Gew 43, but they also impressed numbers of captured SVT40s as the S1Gew 259(r) – examples with the telescopic sight became the S1Gew Zf260(r).

Below top: Early production model of SVT40 with PU telescopic sight. Centre: Carbine version of the SVT40. Bottom: Soviet troops in action with the SVT40

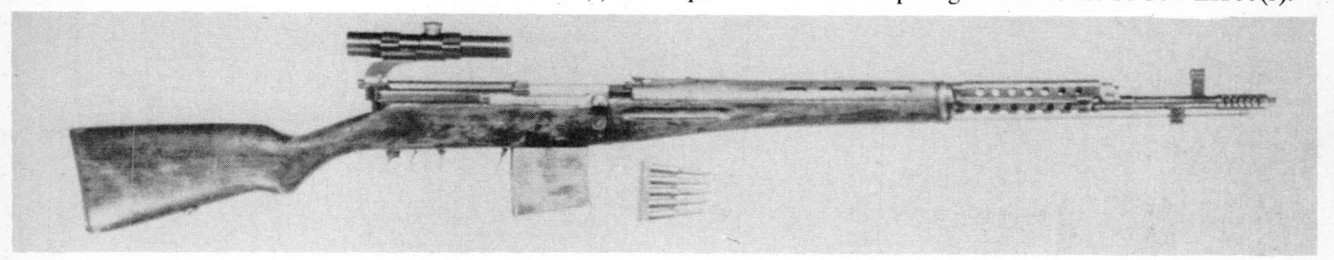

RUSSIAN PORTABLE FLAME-THROWERS

Ranzewüj ognemjot K S-2 (ROKS-2)

Known portable flame-throwers used by the Russian Army during WW2 were the ROKS-2 and ROKS-3. In the case of the ROKS-2, the fuel oil was carried in a rectangular metal container that closely resembled a soldier's normal shoulder pack. The air cylinder was attached horizontally beneath the pack. The flame-gun, or projector, was in the form of a rifle. ROKS-3 consisted of a large fuel tank and a small pressure cylinder, again the flame-gun was in the shape of a rifle.

DATA (ROKS-2)
WEIGHT 22.7 kg 50 lb
FUEL 9 litres 2 gall
RANGE 36.5-45 metres 40-50 yds
DURATION OF FIRE 6-8 seconds

Russian soldier carrying ROKS-3 flame-thrower during the fighting in Budapest

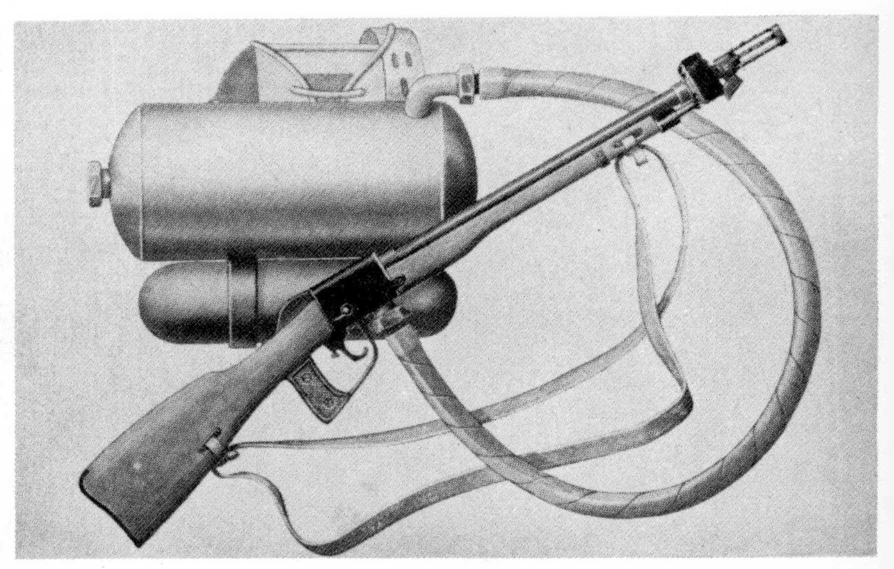

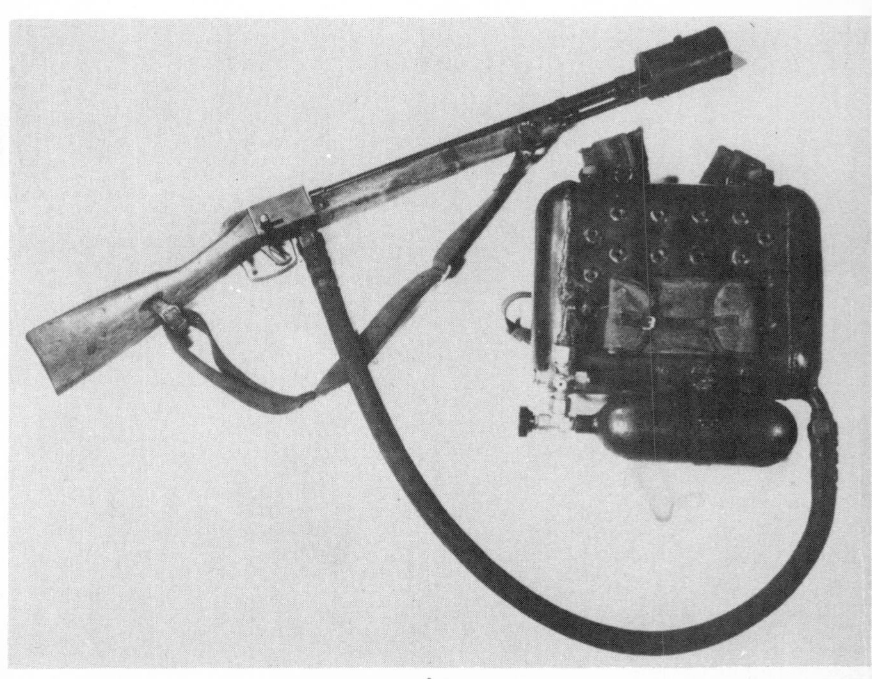

Top right: Ranzewuj ognemjot K S-3

Below right: Ranzewuj ognemjot K S-2

WORLD WAR 2 FACT FILES

This new series, prepared by experts who edit the world's foremost military, naval and aviation reference books, covers the fighting forces of the principal countries which took part in the Second World War. Each study provides a readable narrative supplemented by separate sections on technical details of weaponry, logistics and general administration that are seldom given in campaign and battle studies.

ANTI-TANK WEAPONS
MACHINE GUNS
BRITISH ESCORT SHIPS
AMERICAN GUNBOATS AND MINESWEEPERS
MORTARS AND ROCKETS
ANTI-AIRCRAFT GUNS
INFANTRY, MOUNTAIN AND AIRBORNE GUNS
LIGHT AND MEDIUM FIELD ARTILLERY
SELF-PROPELLED ANTI-TANK AND ANTI-AIRCRAFT GUNS
HEAVY ARTILLERY
AXIS PISTOLS, RIFLES AND GRENADES
ALLIED PISTOLS, RIFLES AND GRENADES

WW2 Aircraft Fact Files

U.S. NAVY AND MARINE CORPS FIGHTERS
JAPANESE ARMY FIGHTERS (PART 1)
SOVIET AIR FORCE FIGHTERS (PART 1)
U.S. ARMY AIR FORCE FIGHTERS (PART 1)